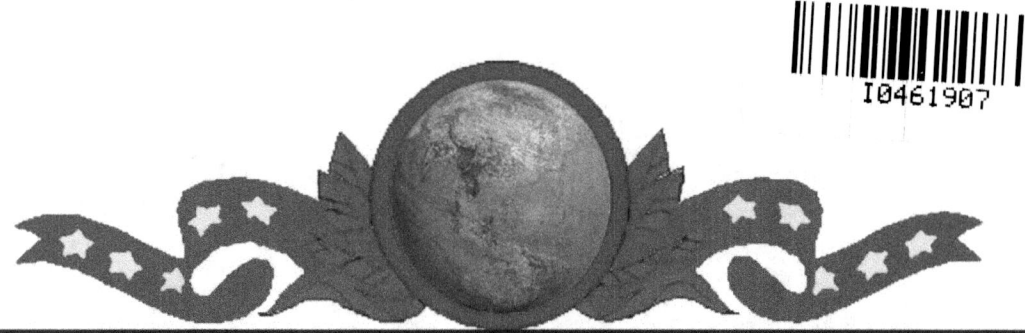

Real World
Colouring Book
For Advanced Users & Adults

Copyright 2019 By John Boom

50 Images

Created From Real Life Photos
For You To Colour As You Please.

ISBN 978-0-359-97230-2

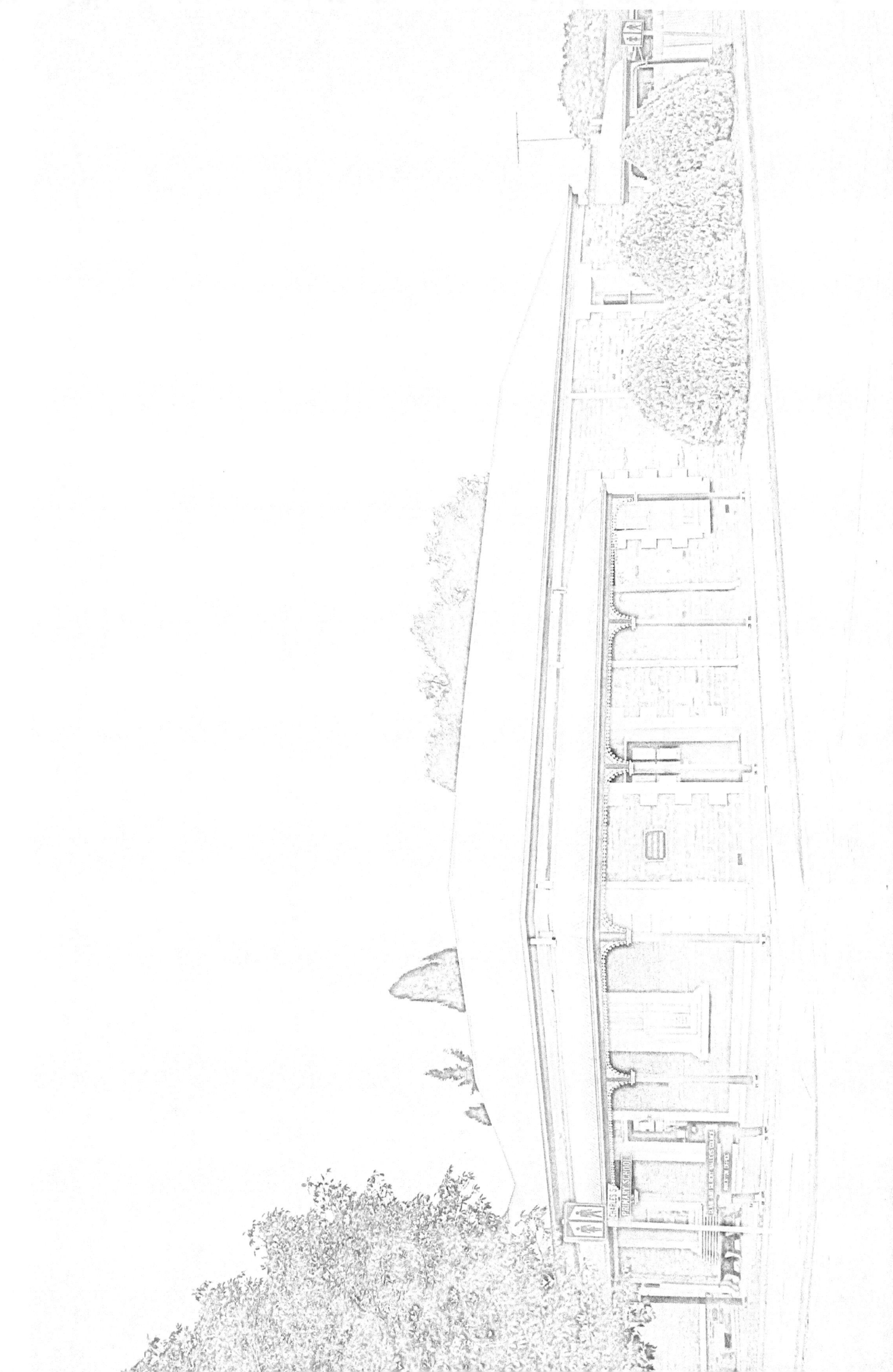

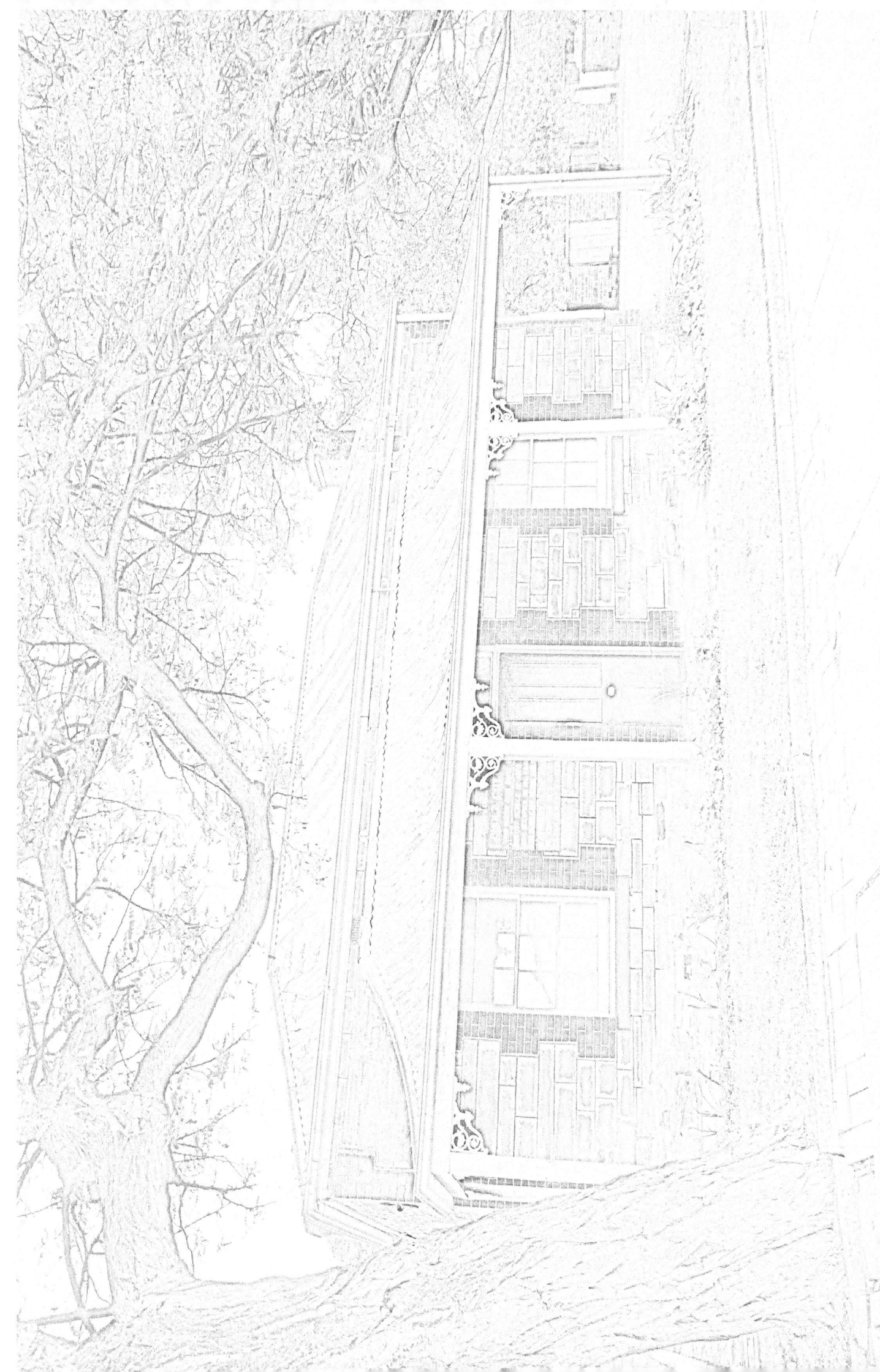

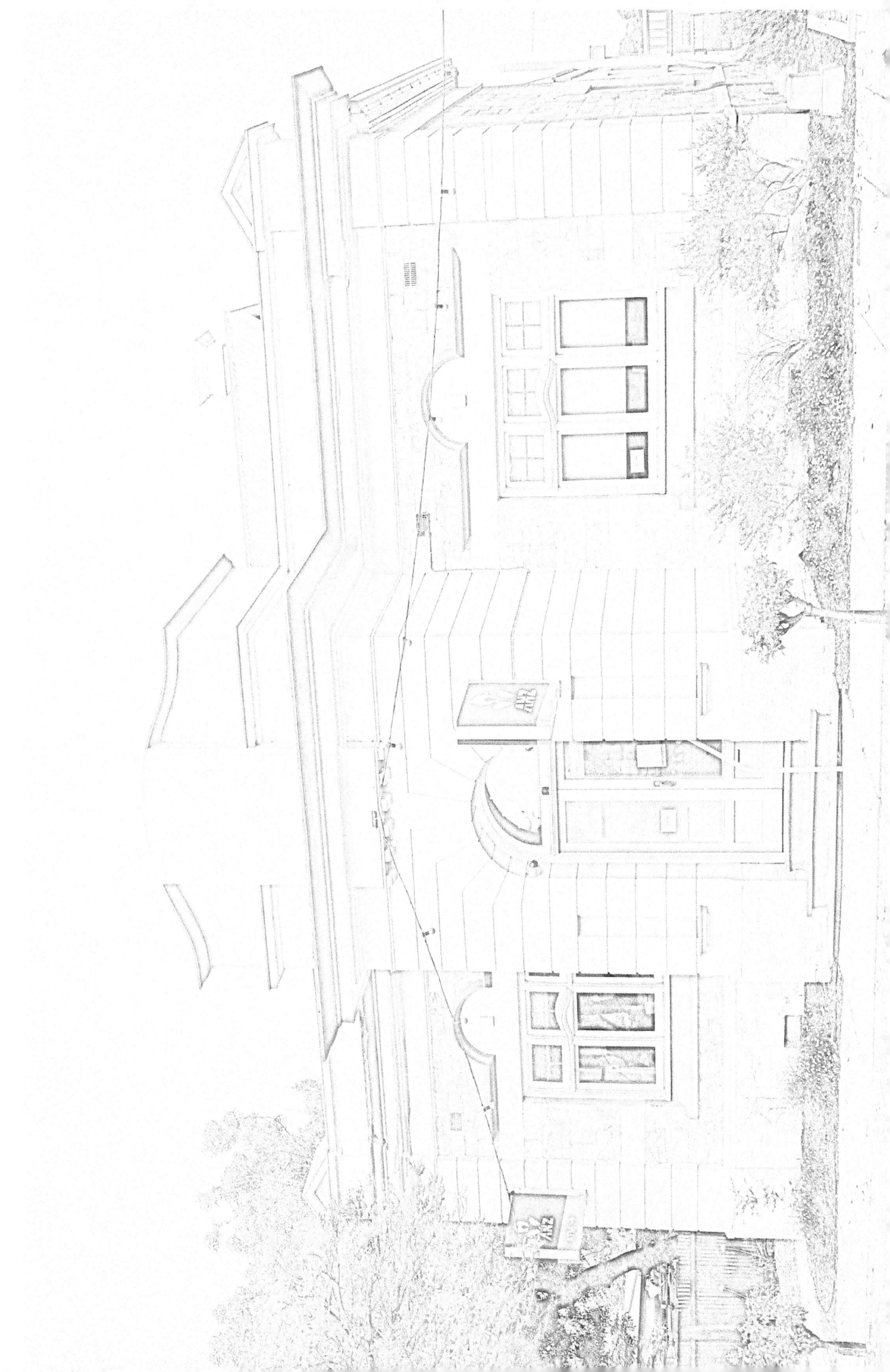

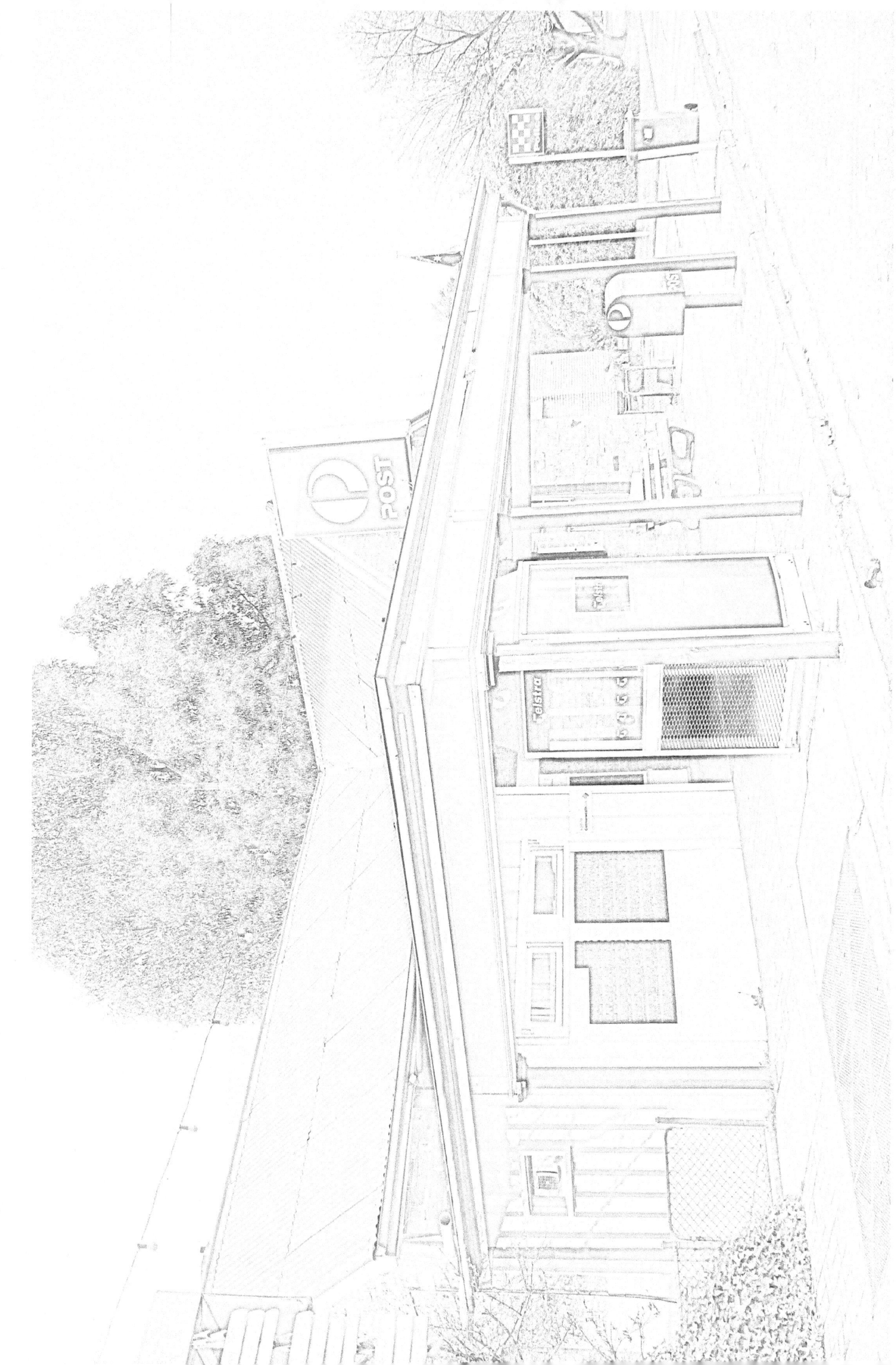

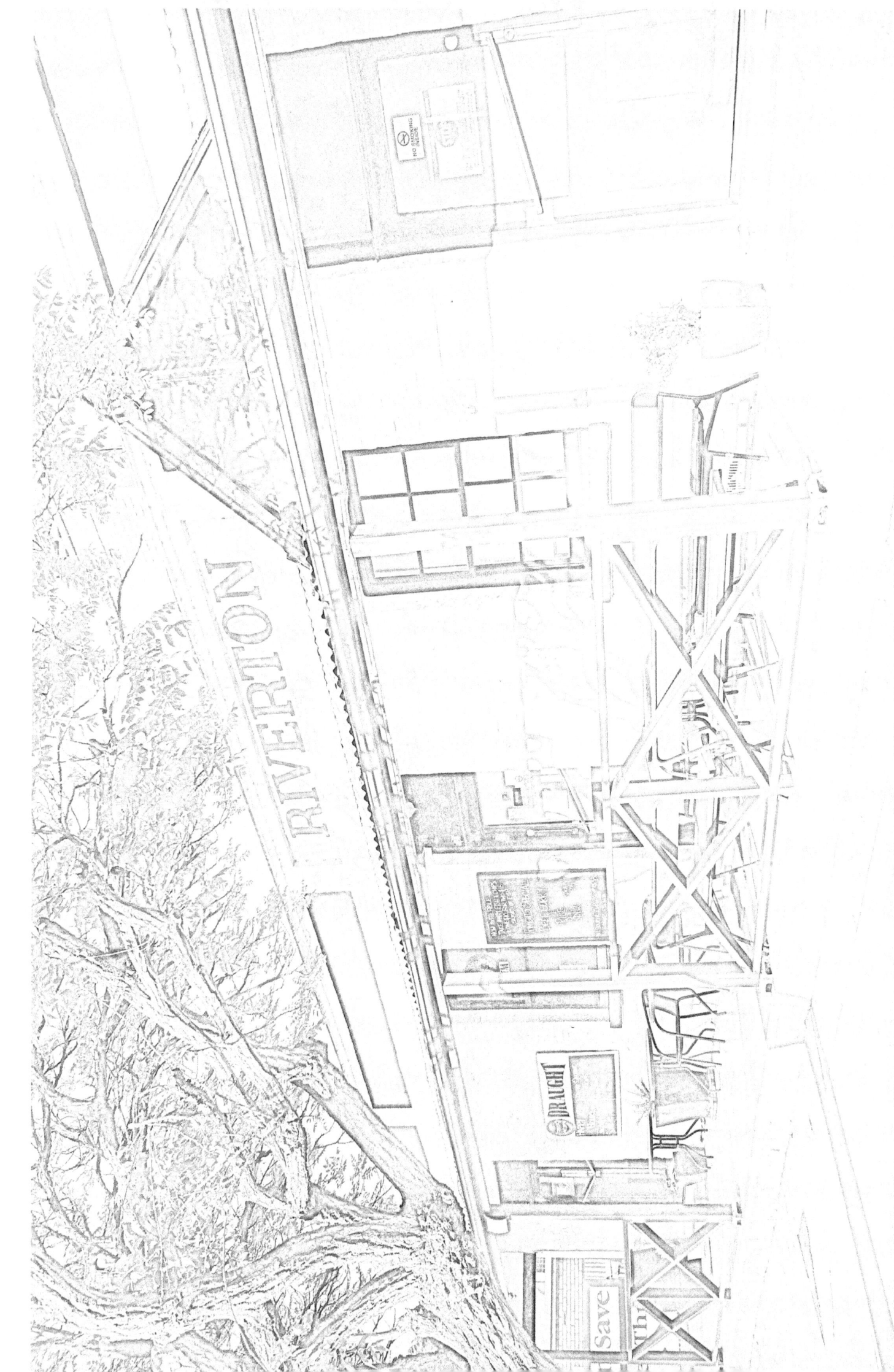

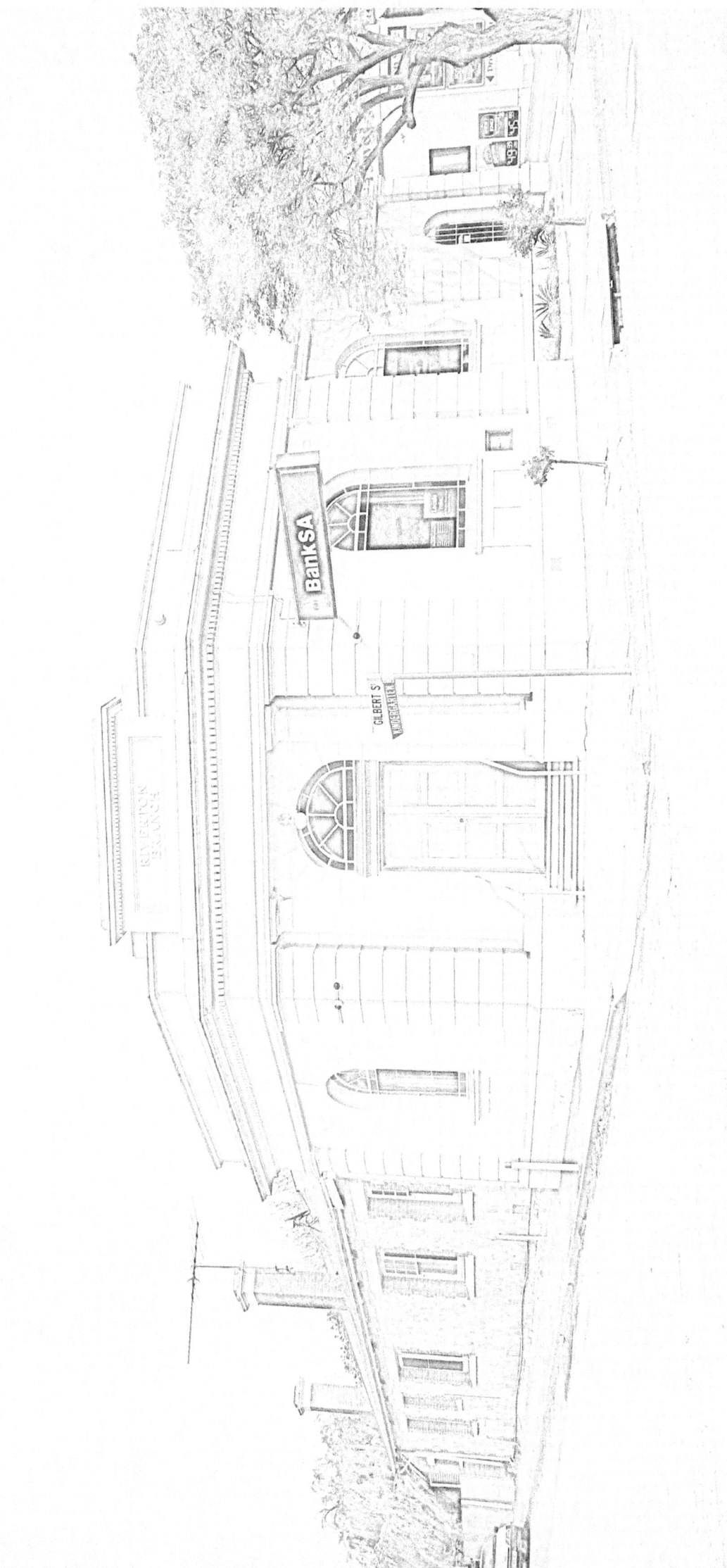

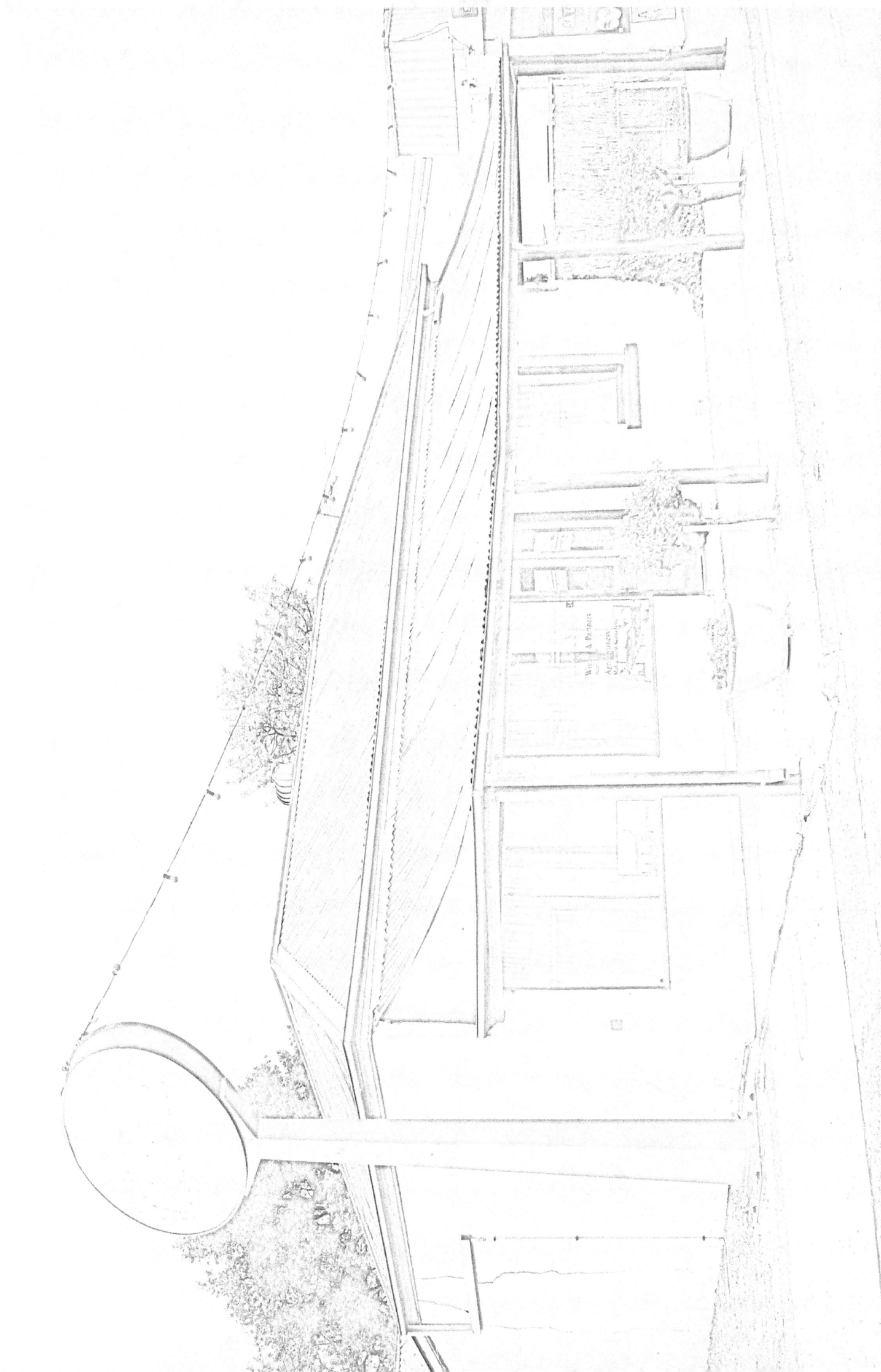

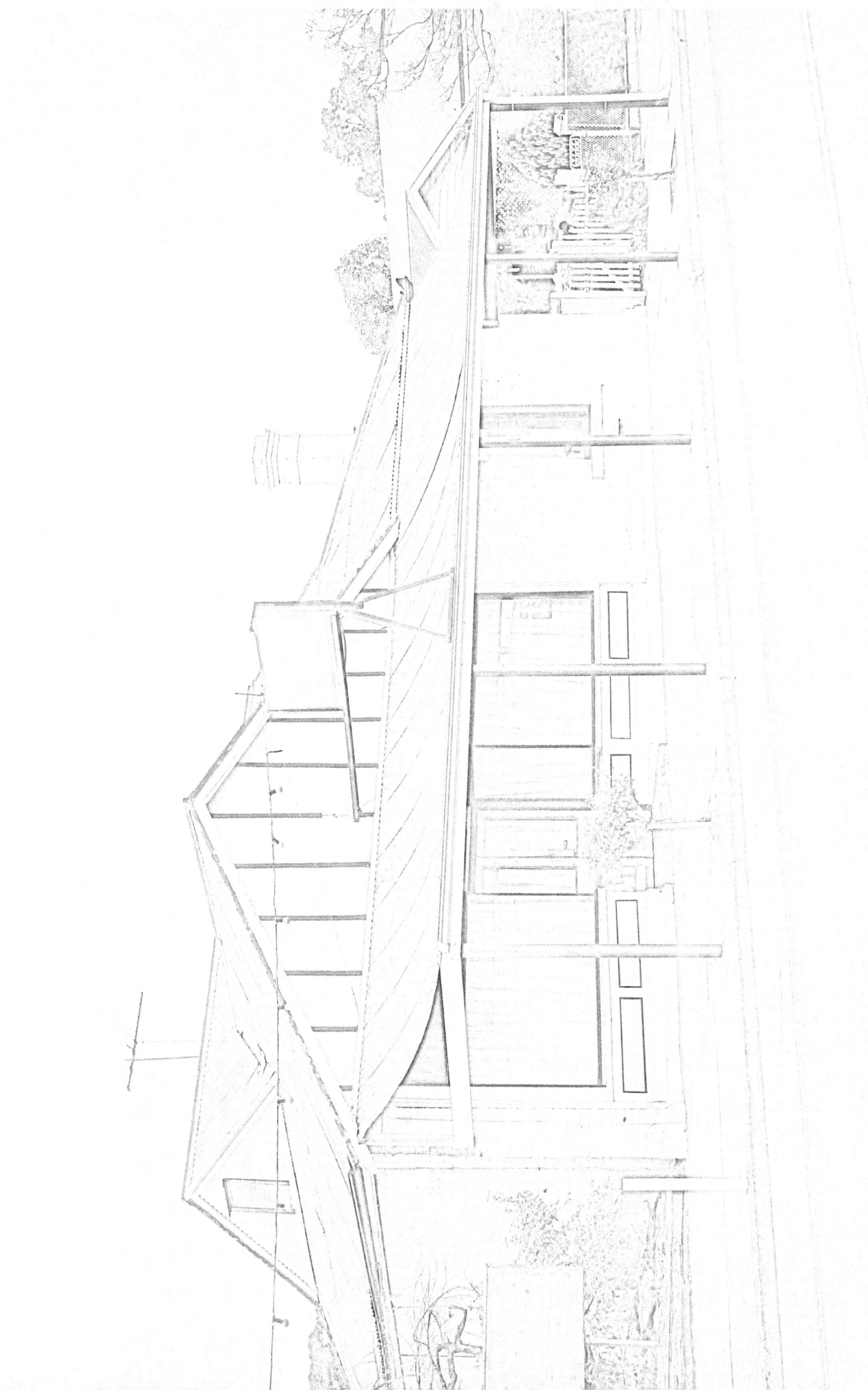

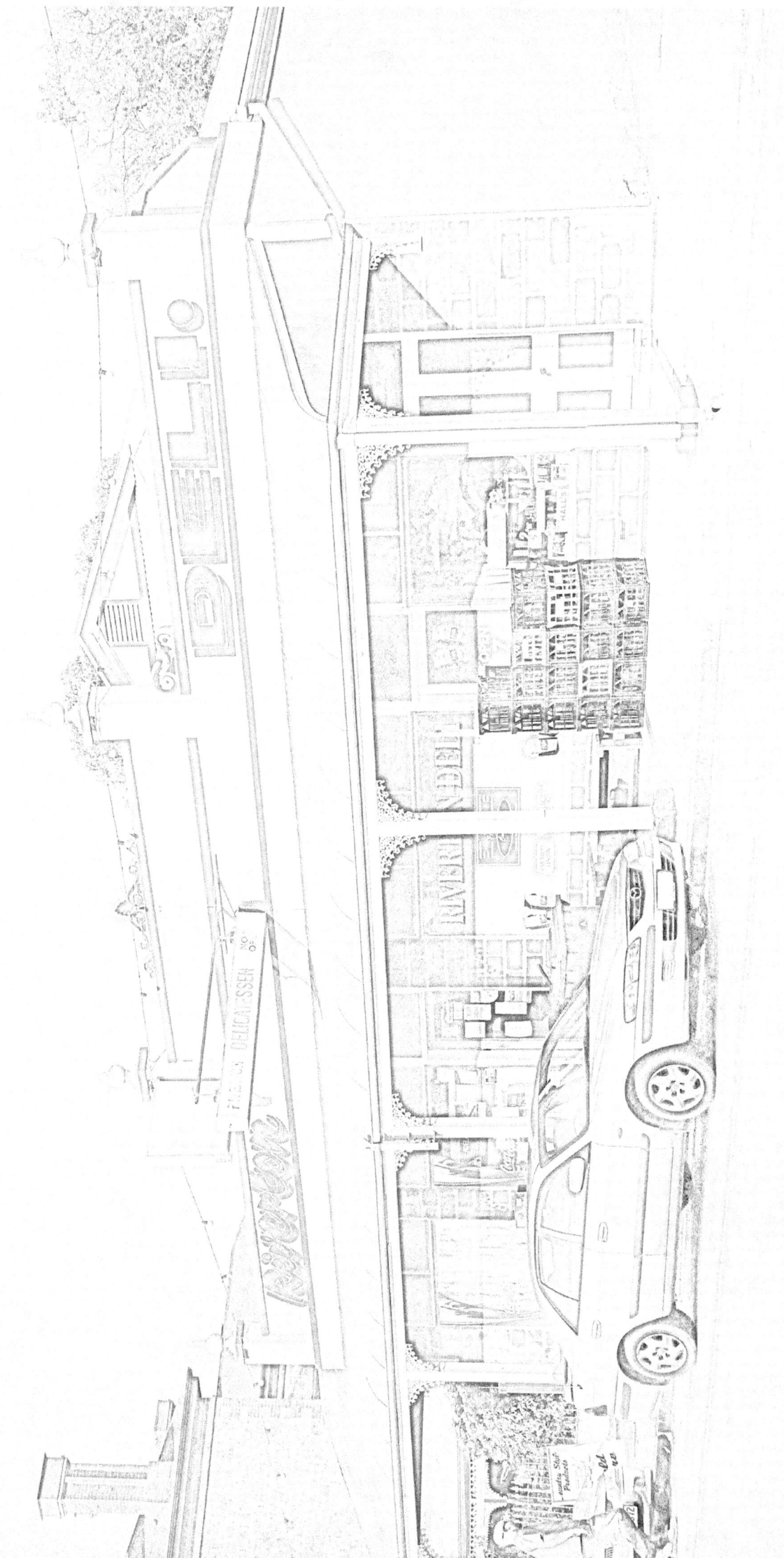

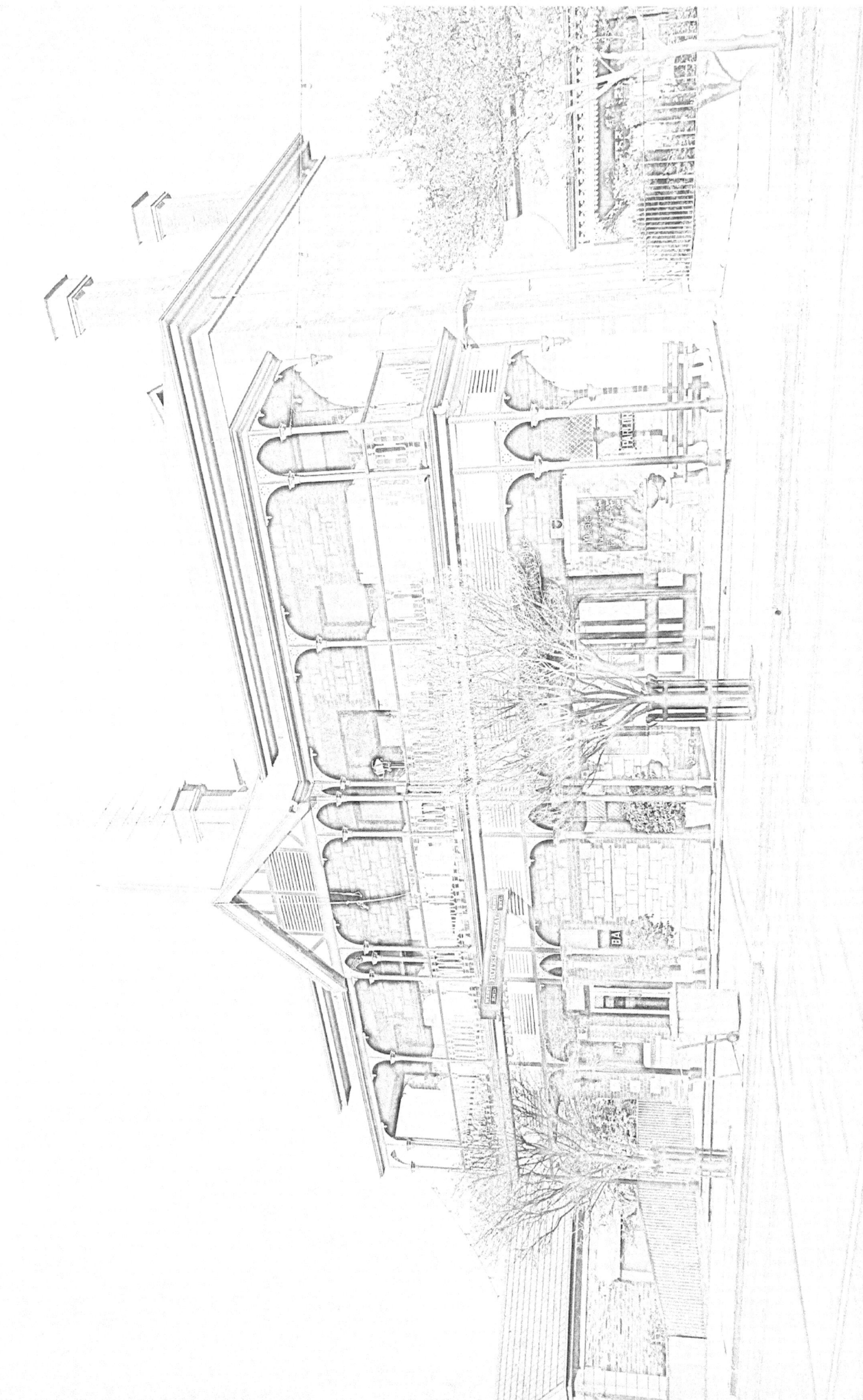

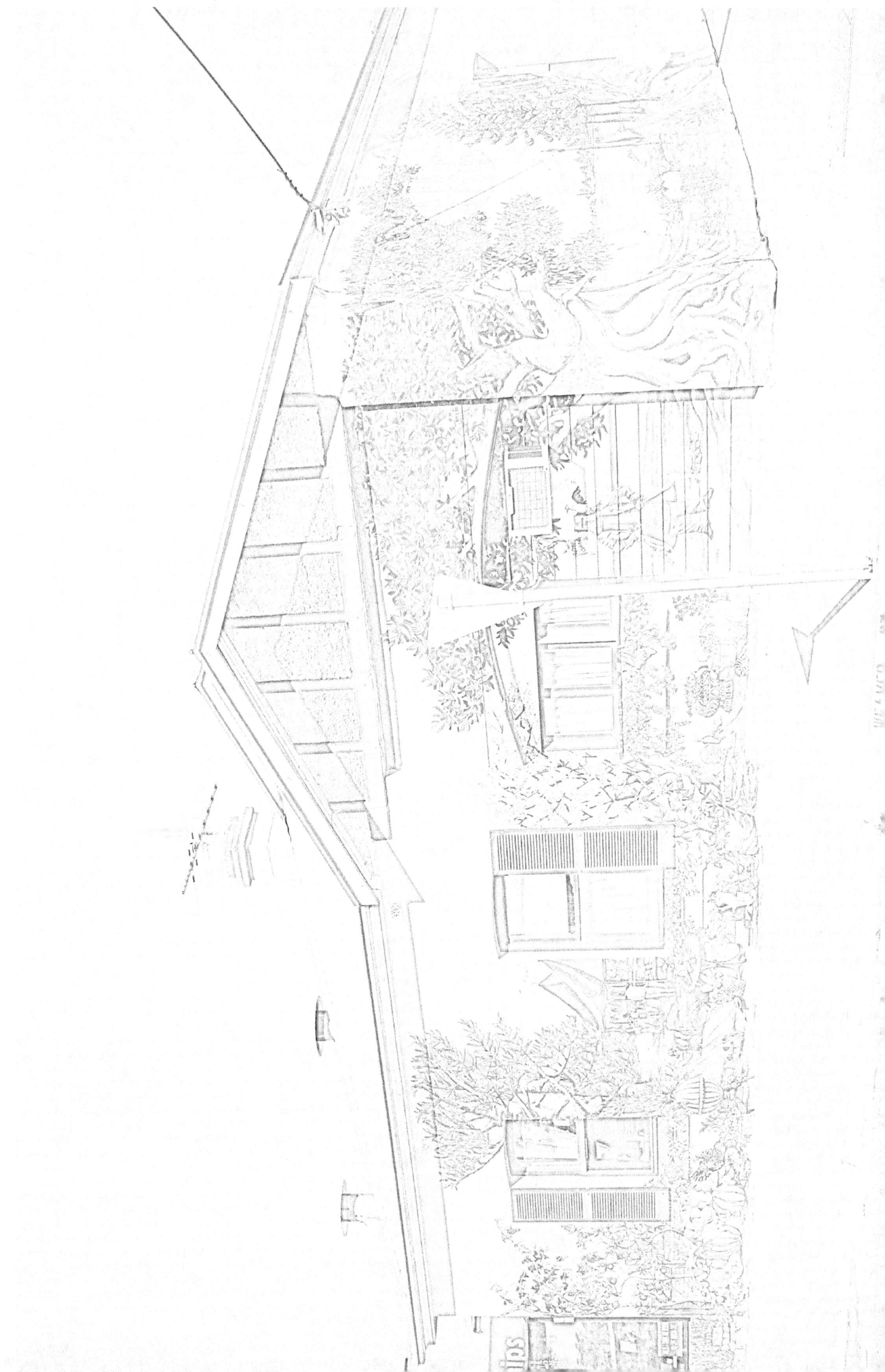

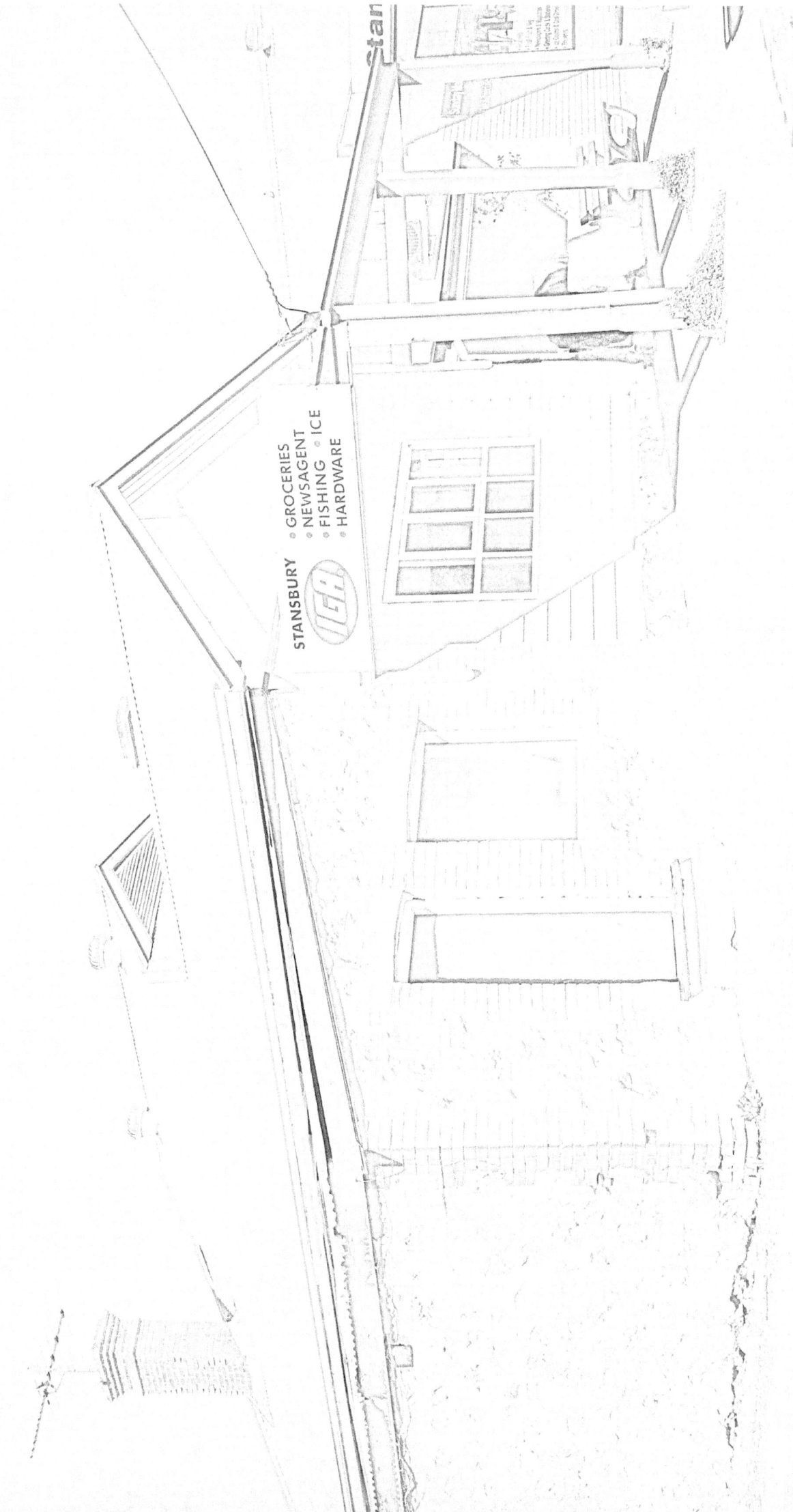

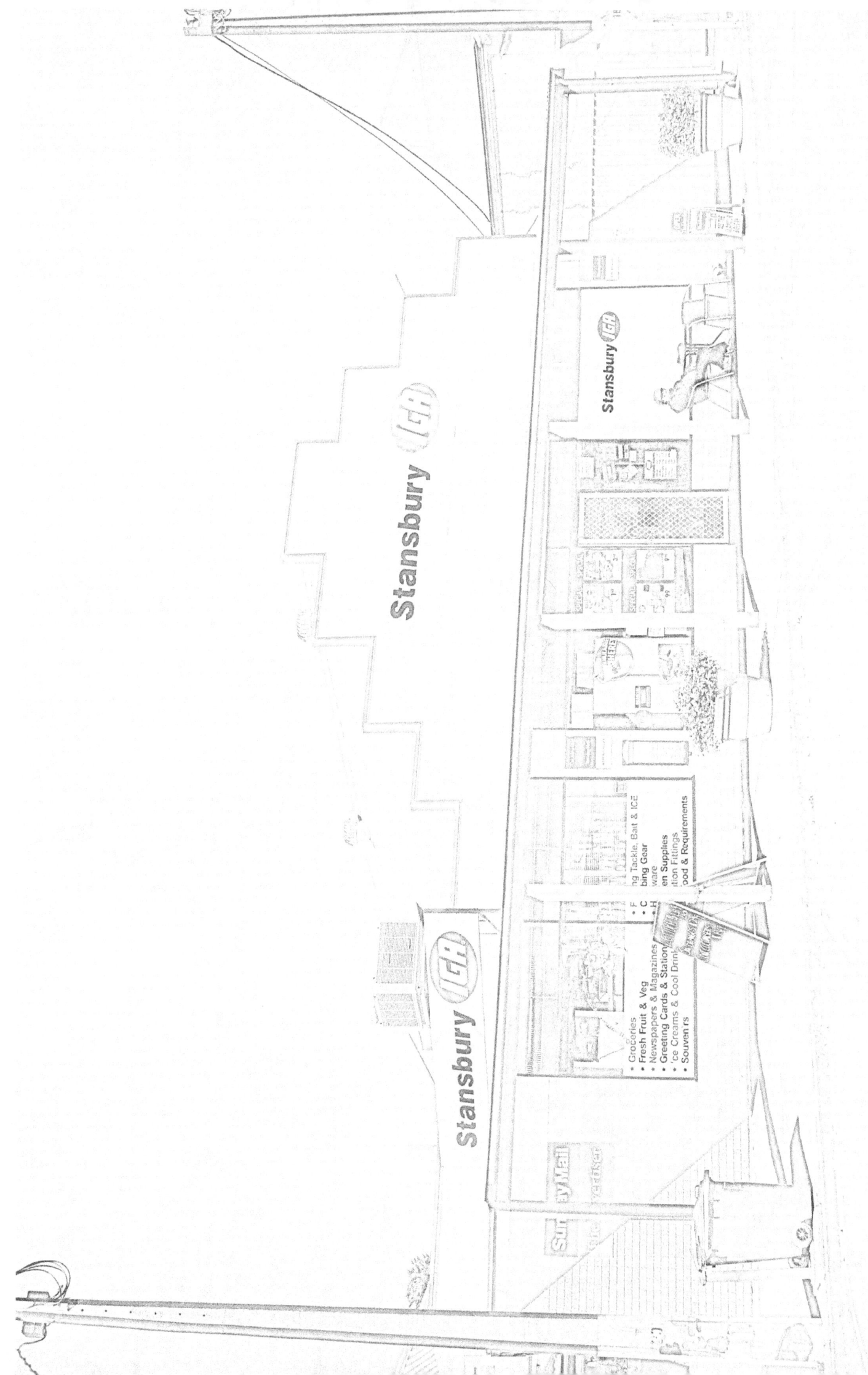

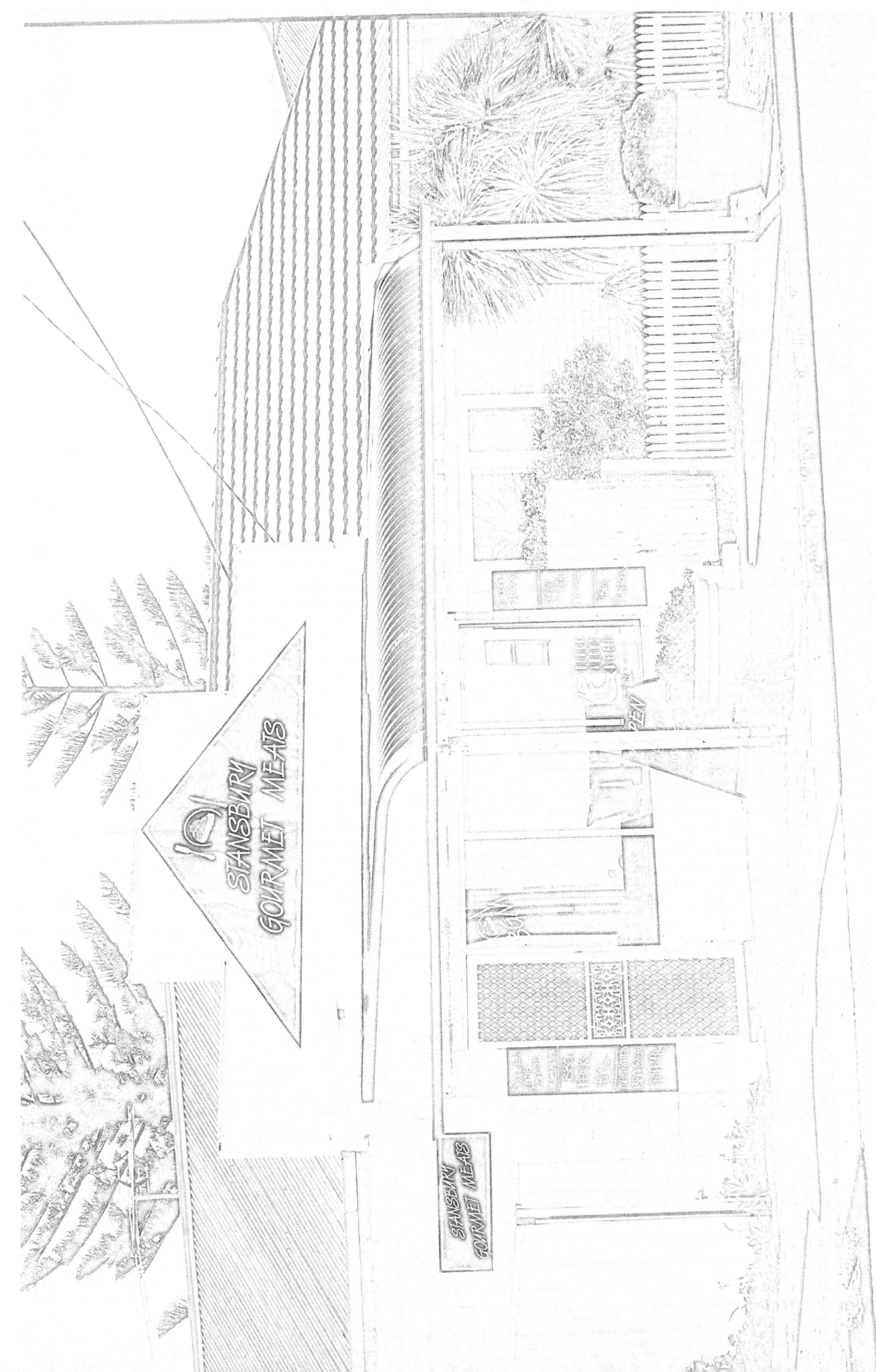

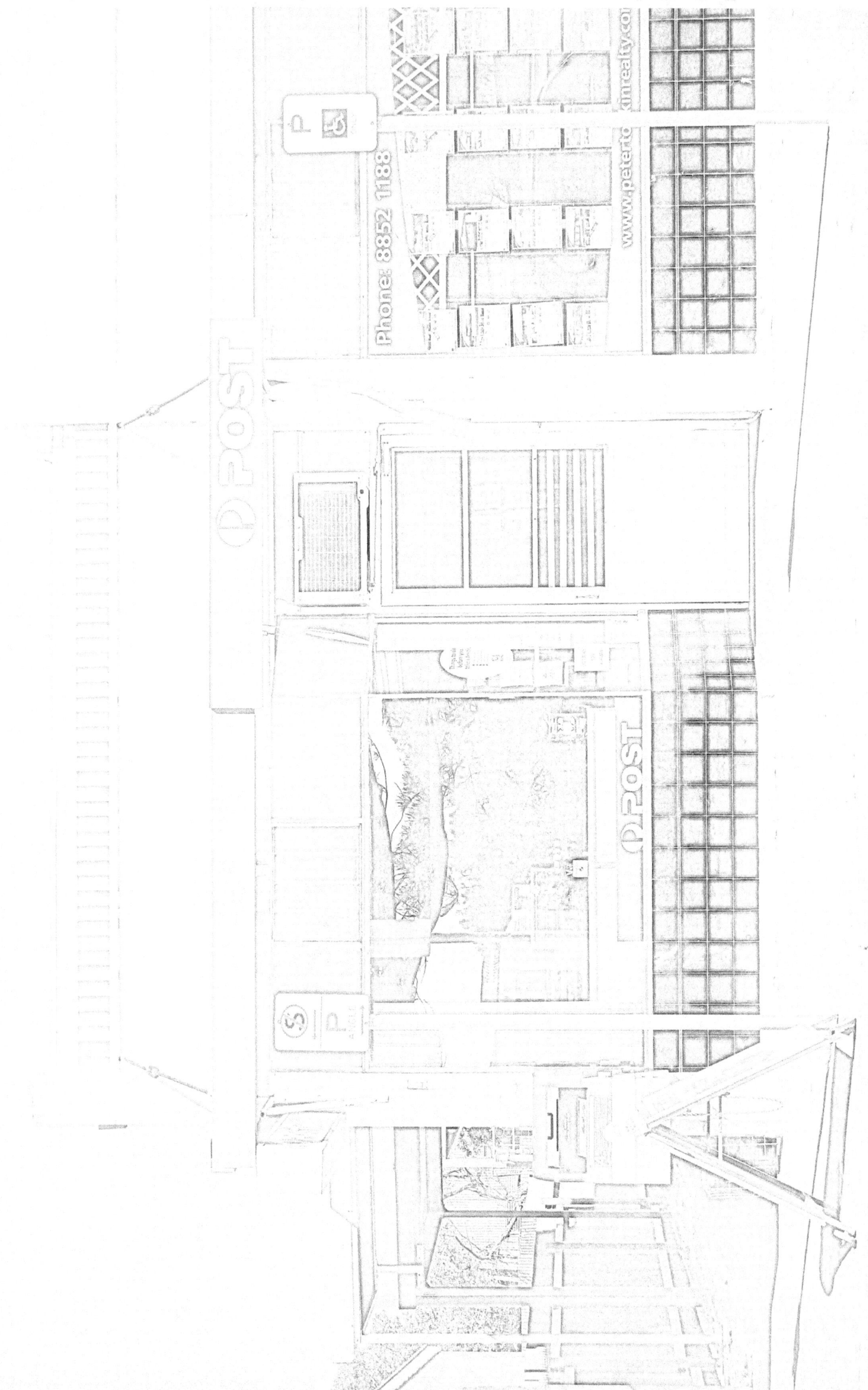

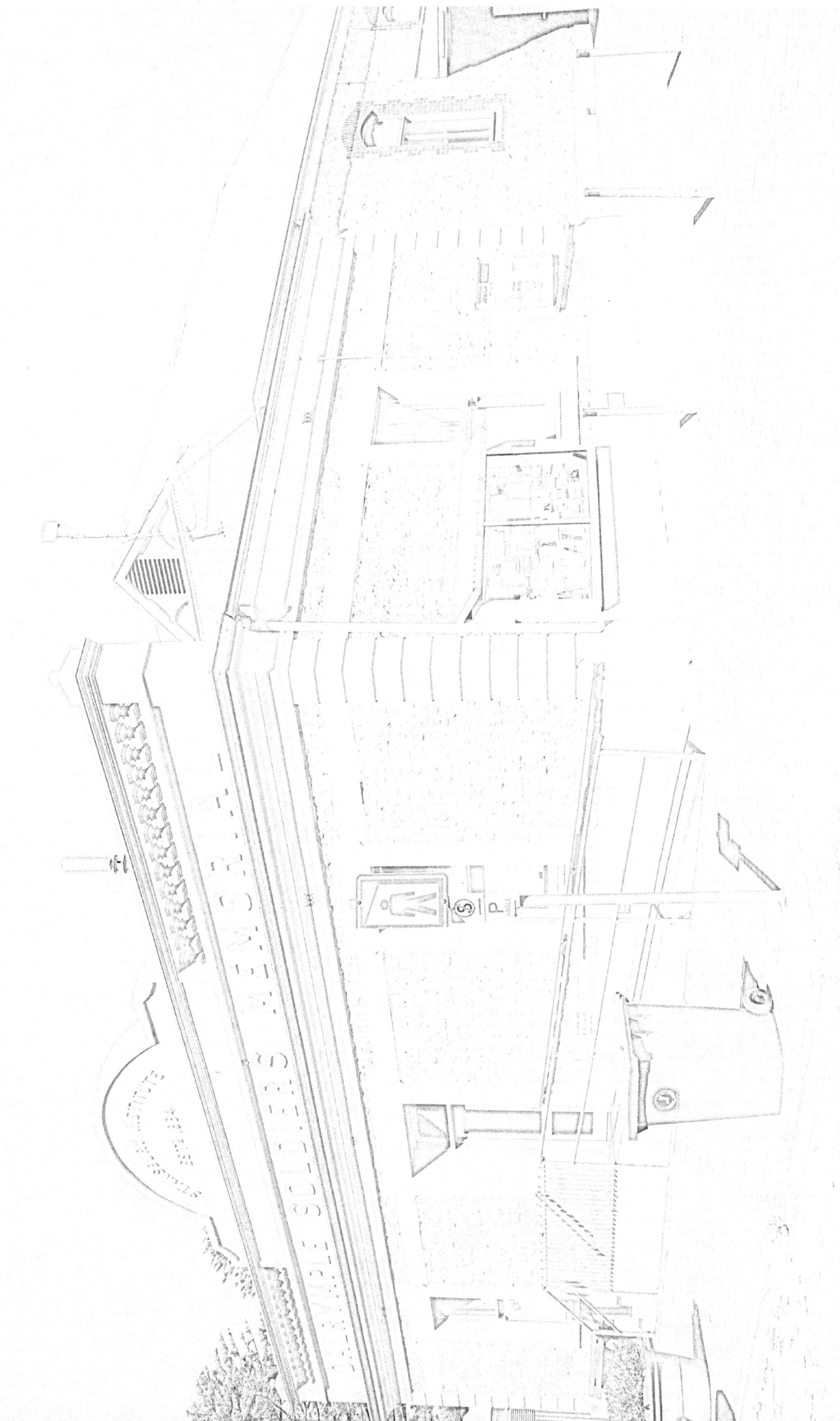

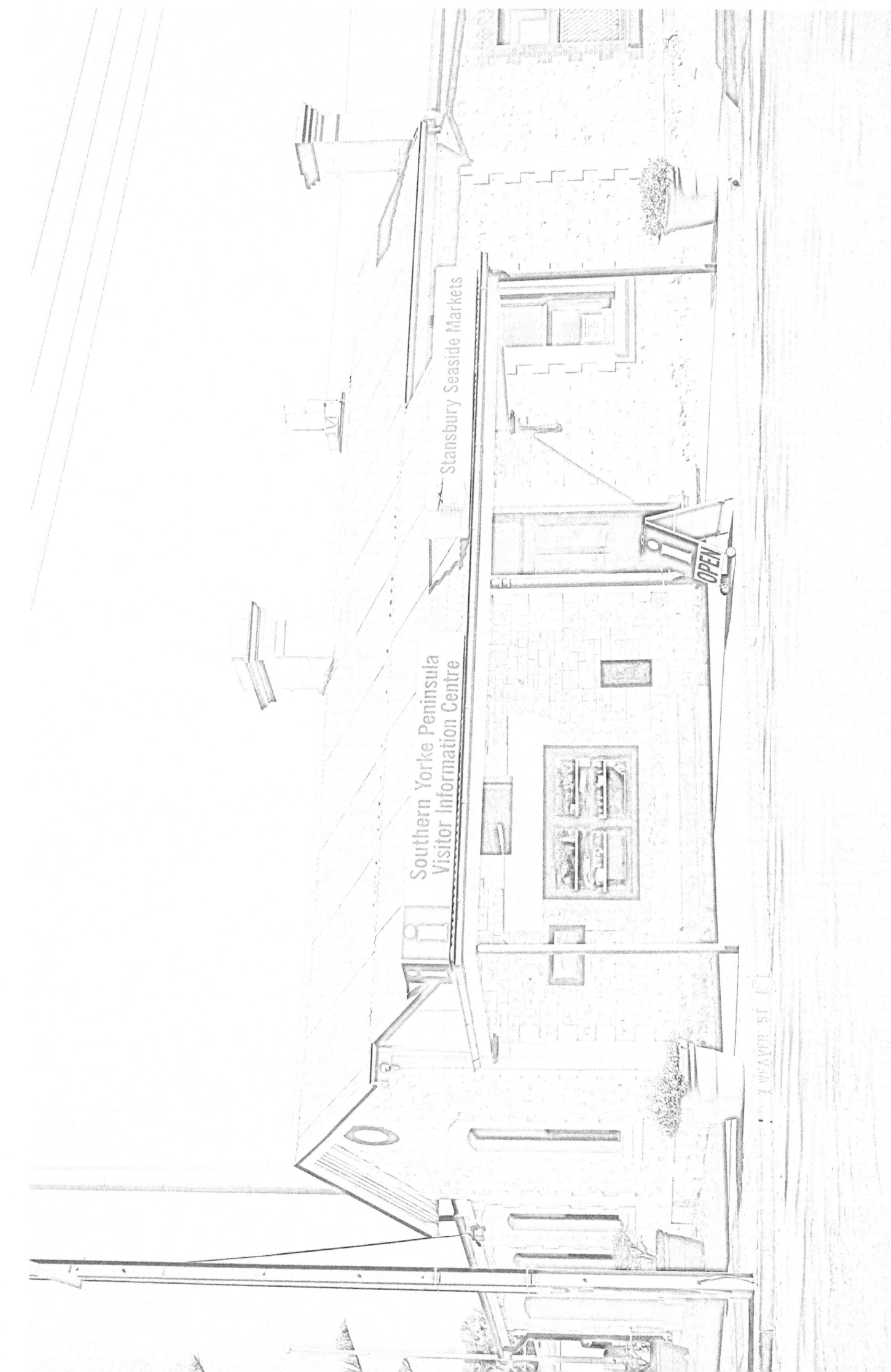

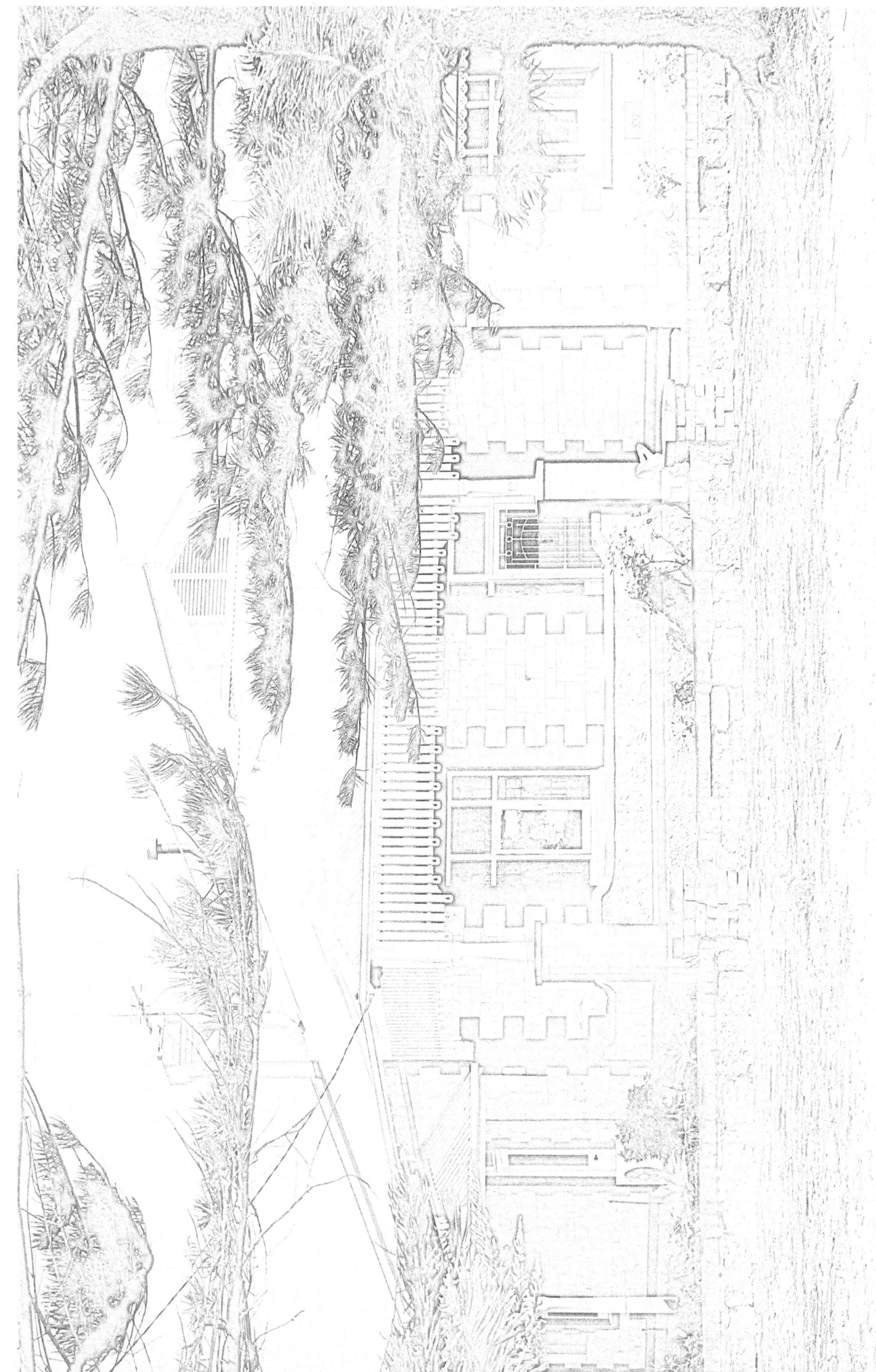

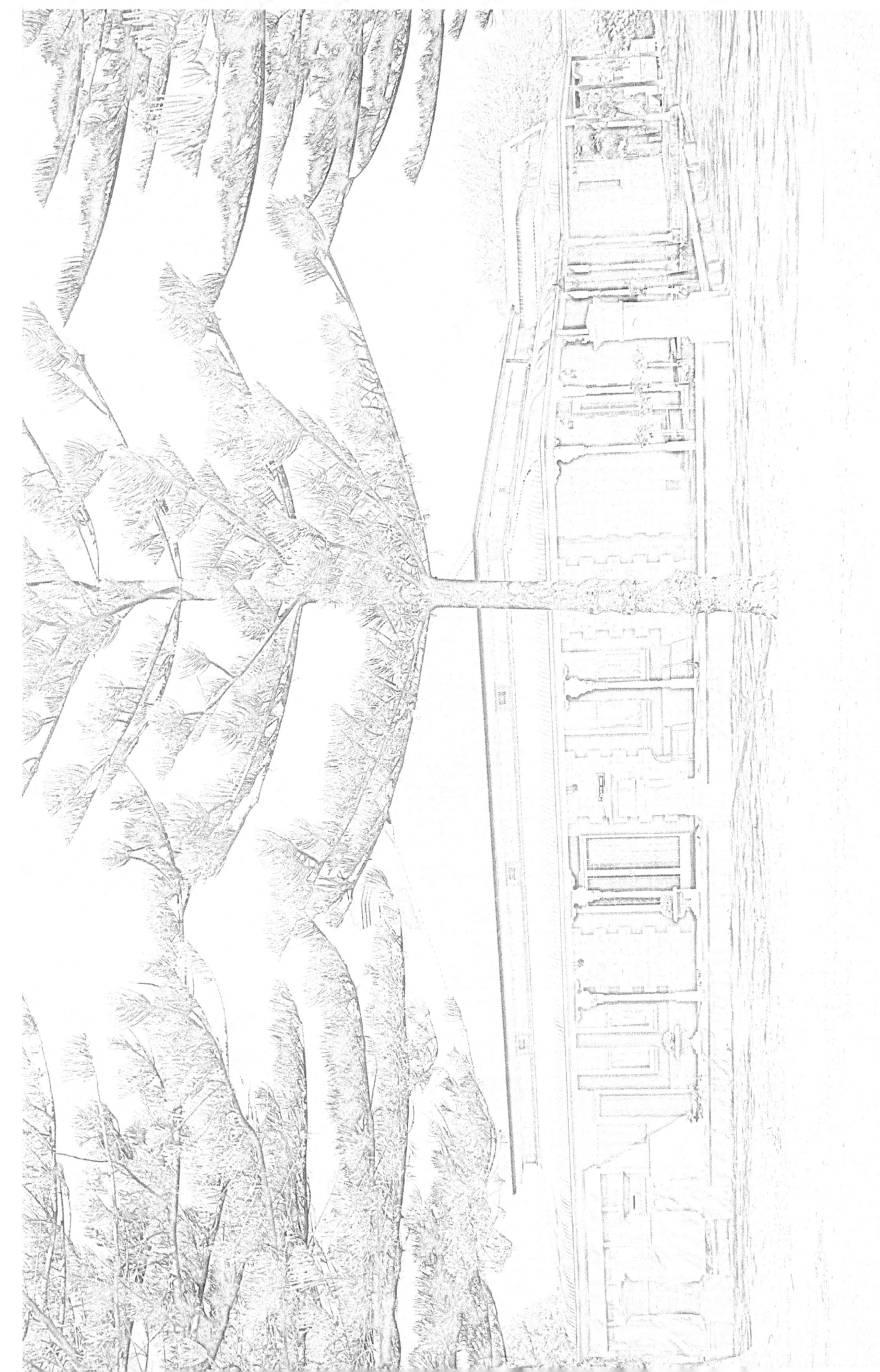

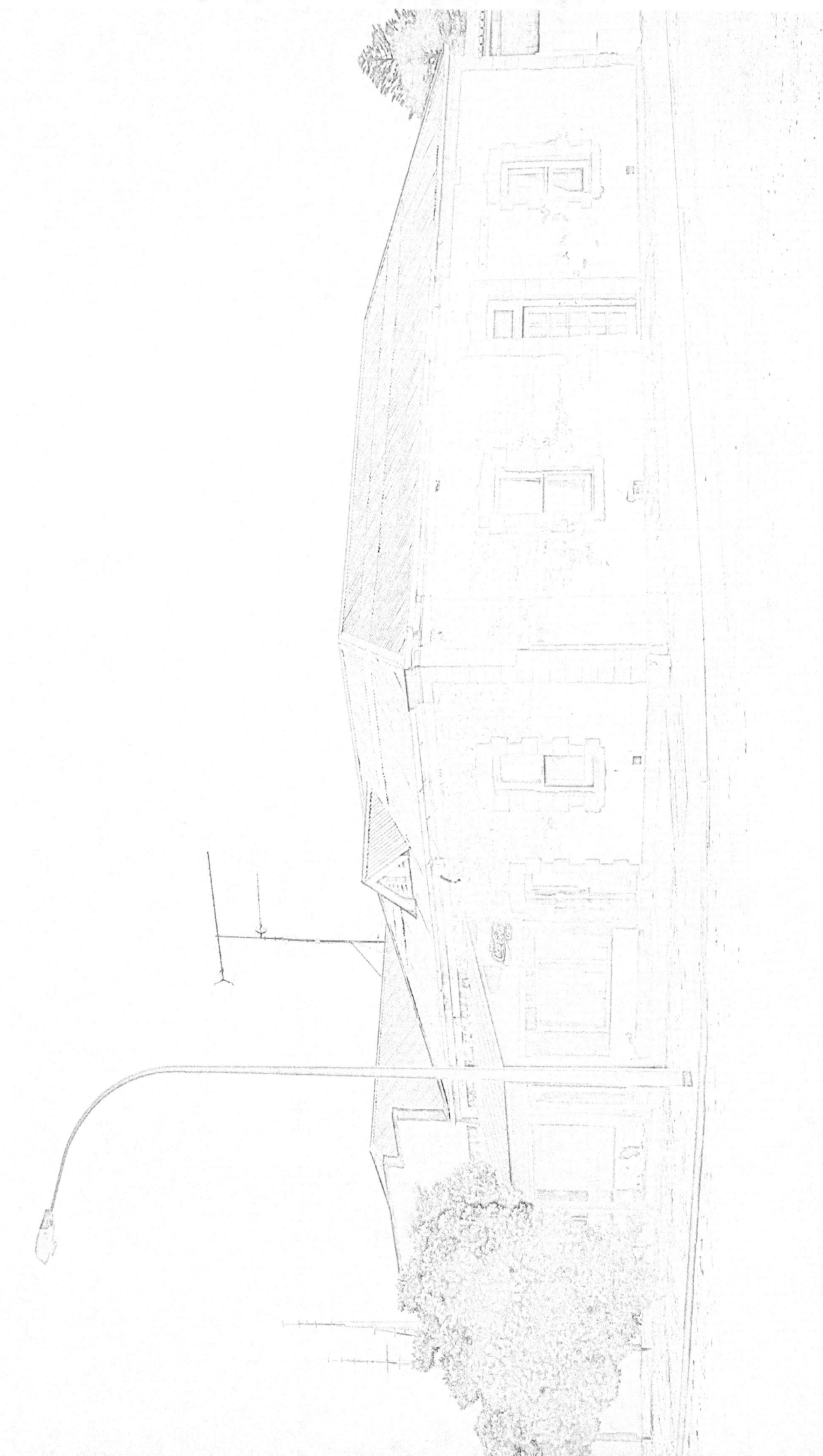

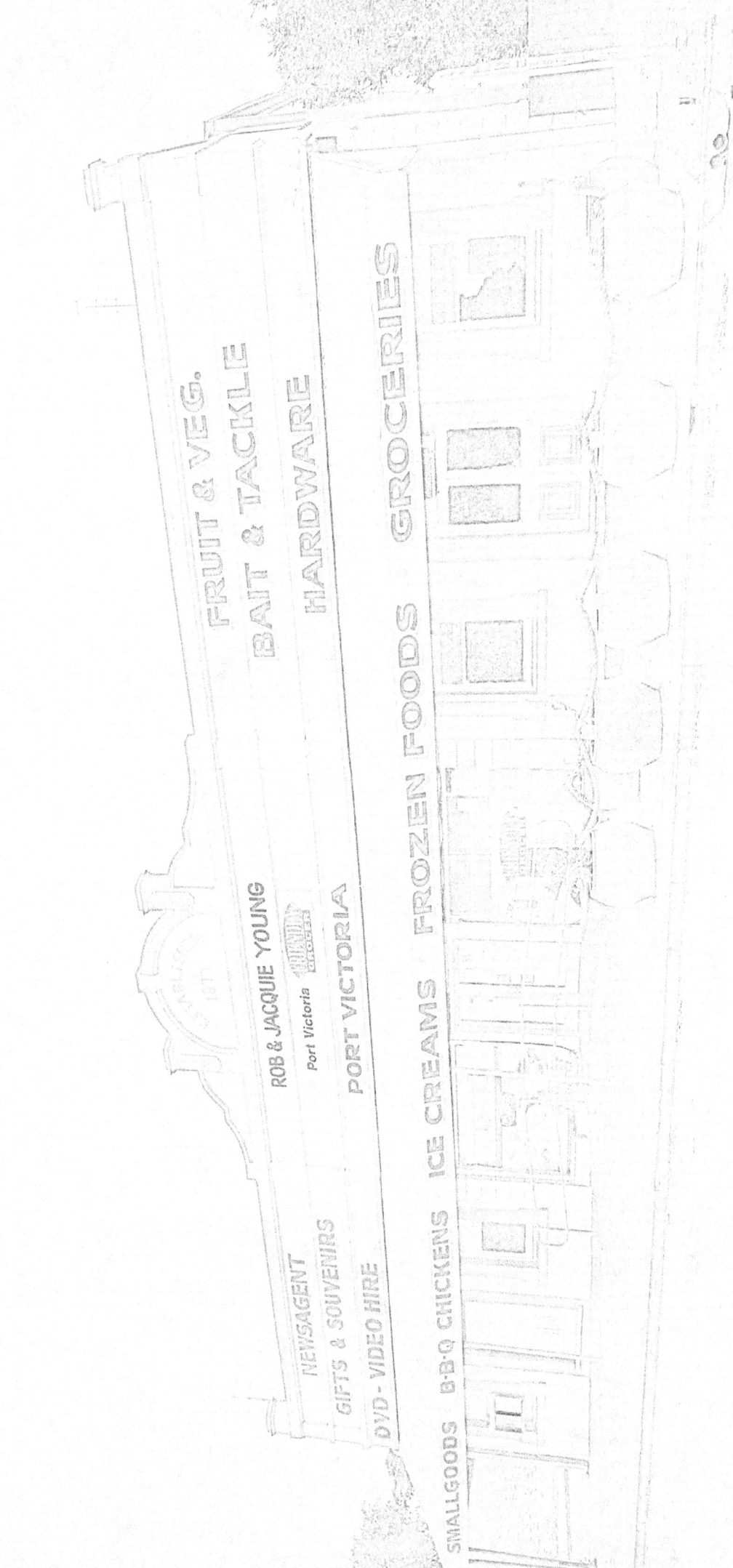

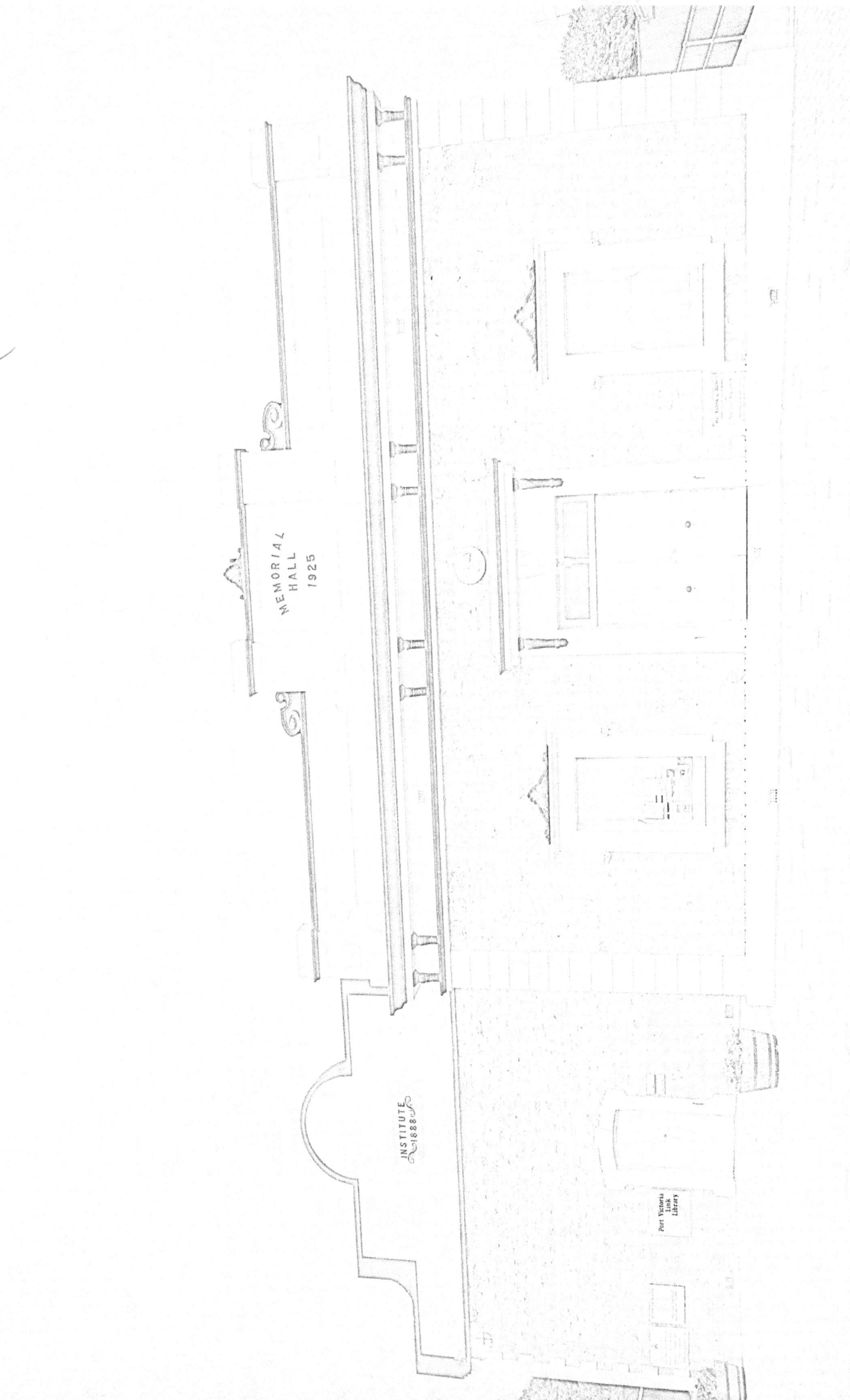

MEMORIAL
HALL
1925

INSTITUTE
1888

Port Victoria
Link
Library

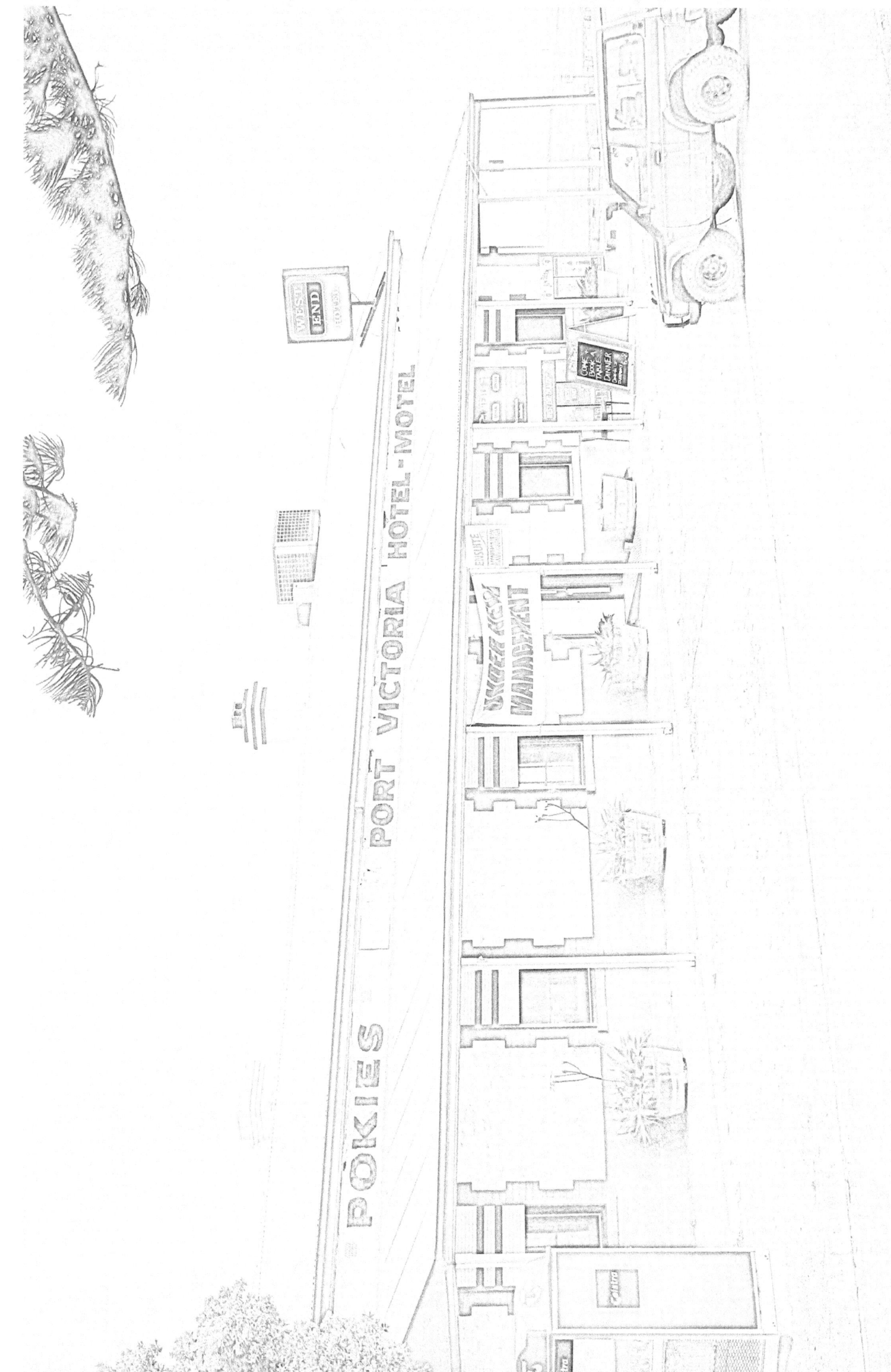

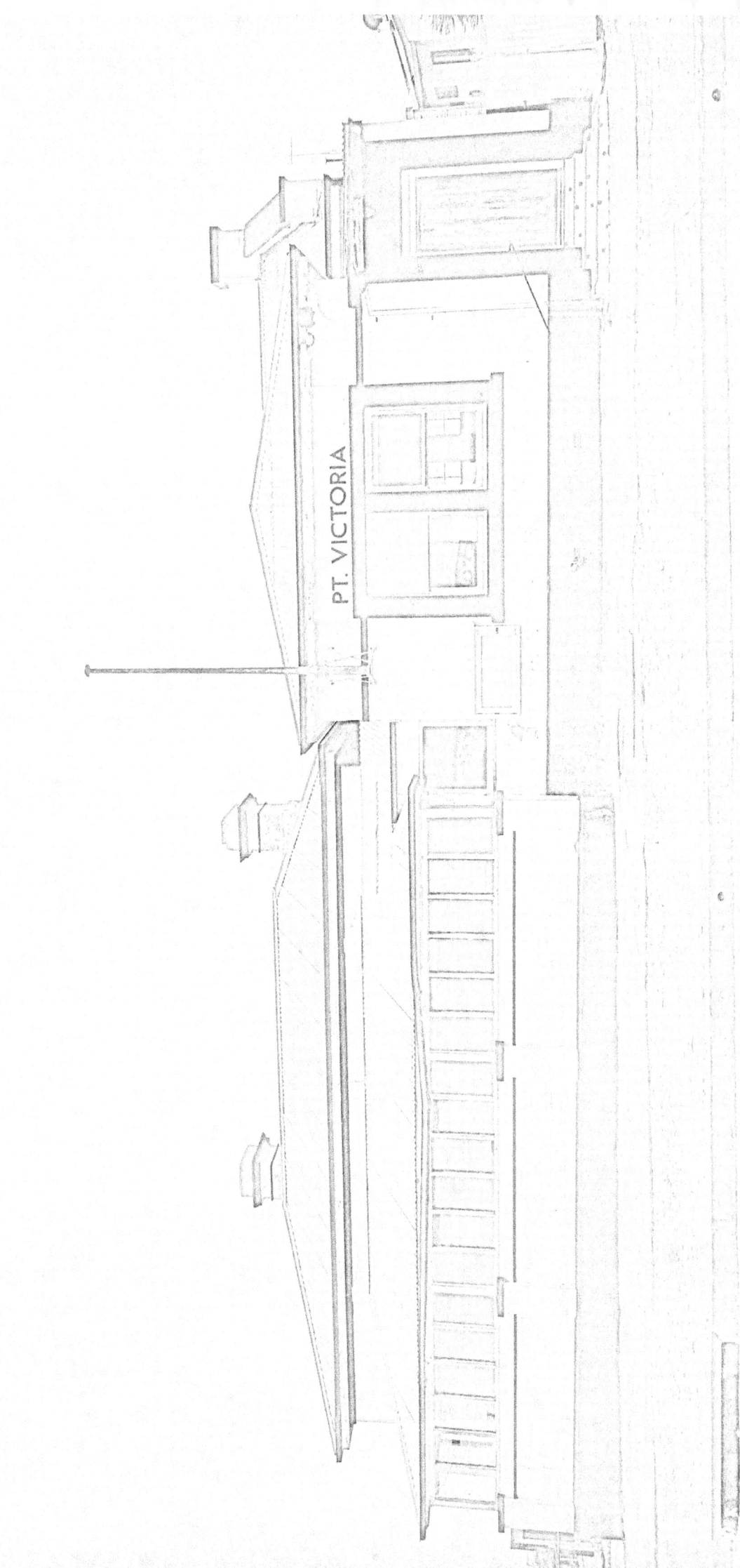

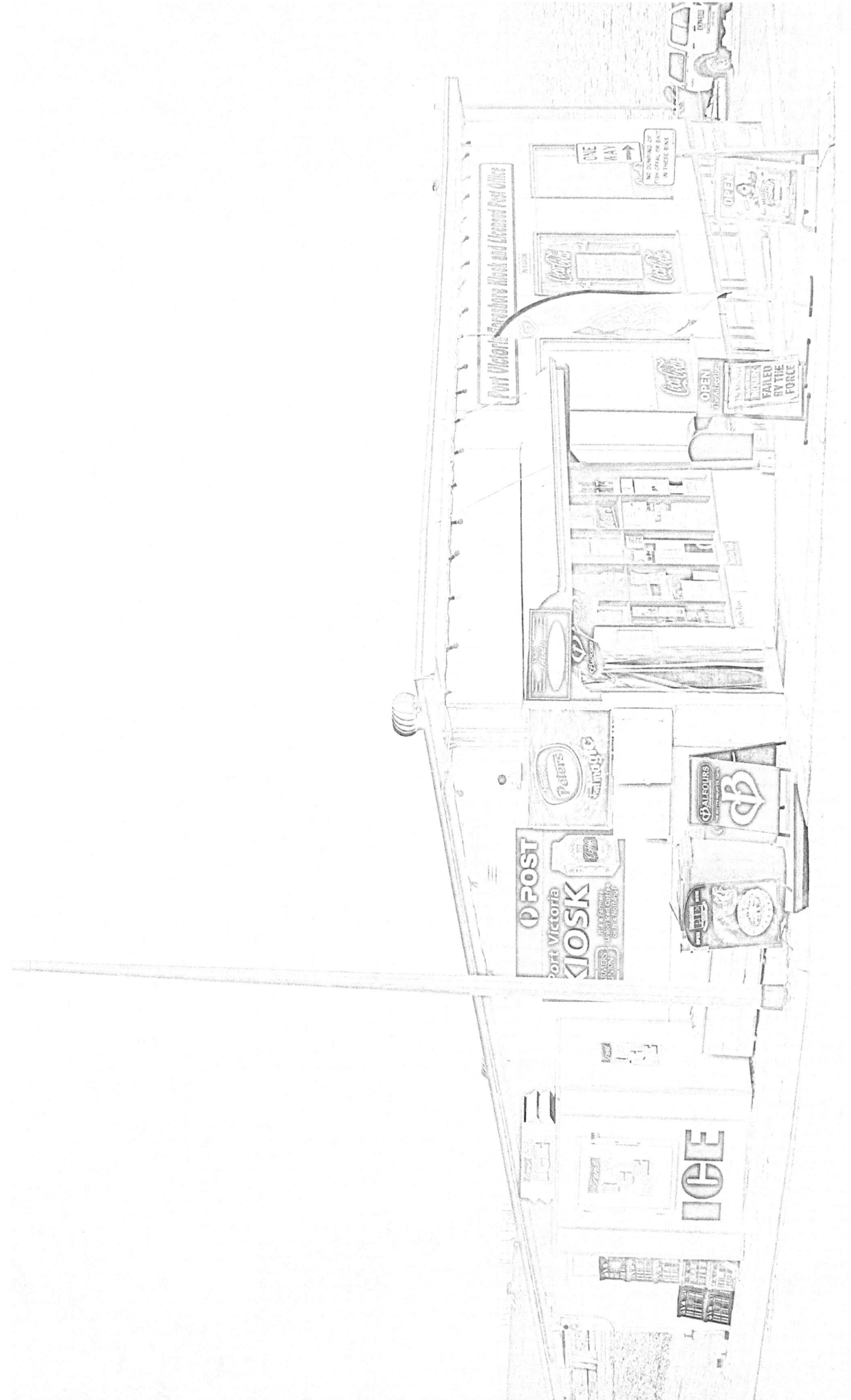

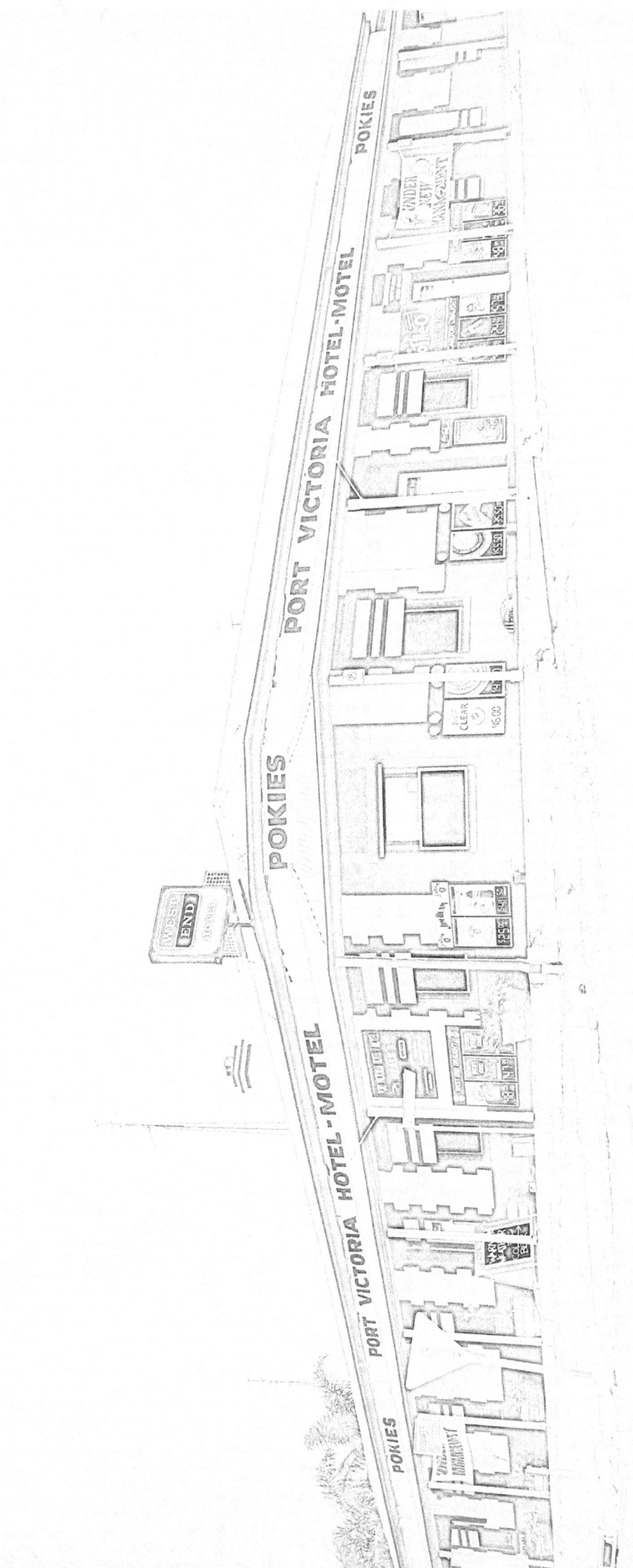

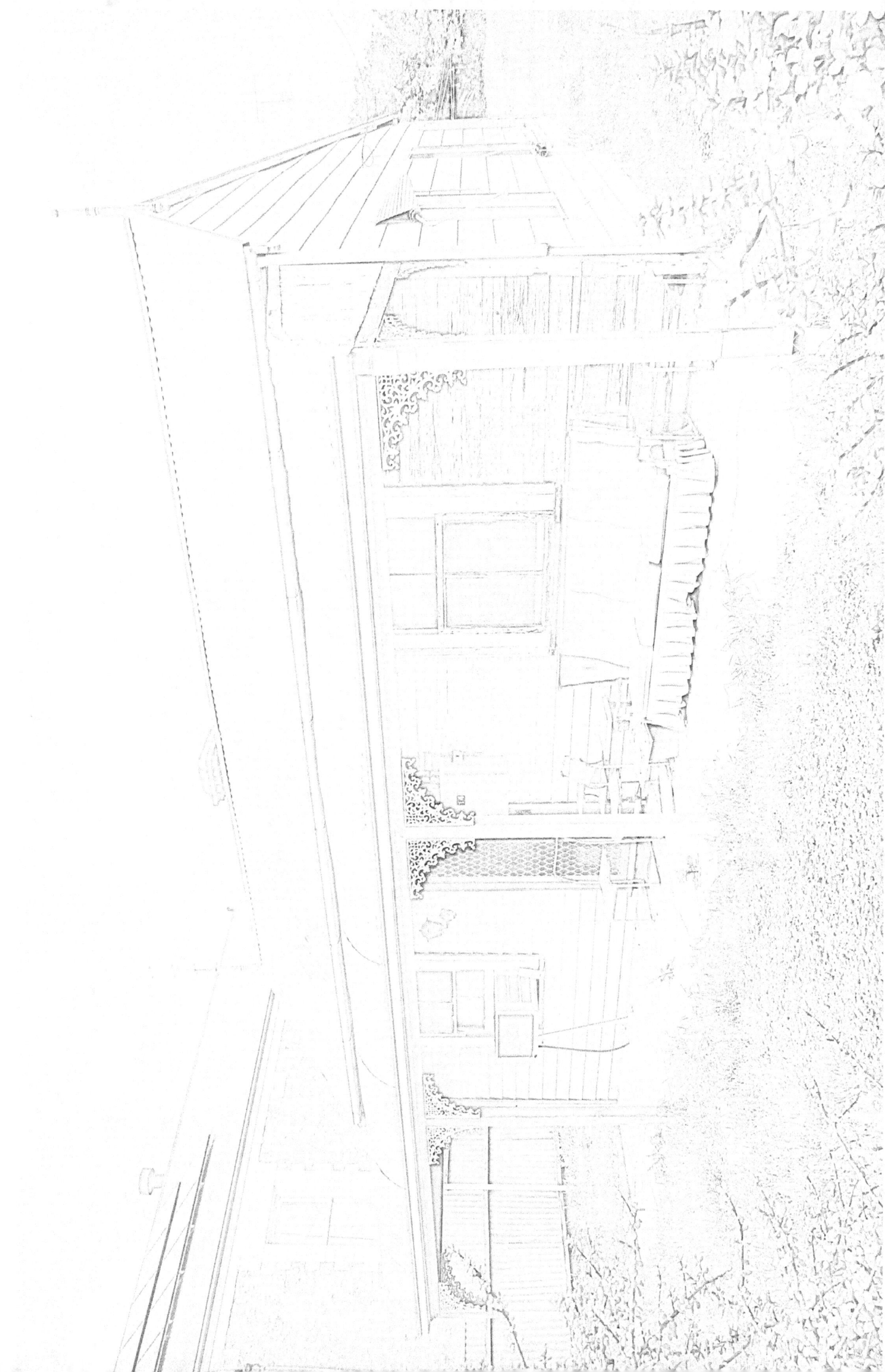

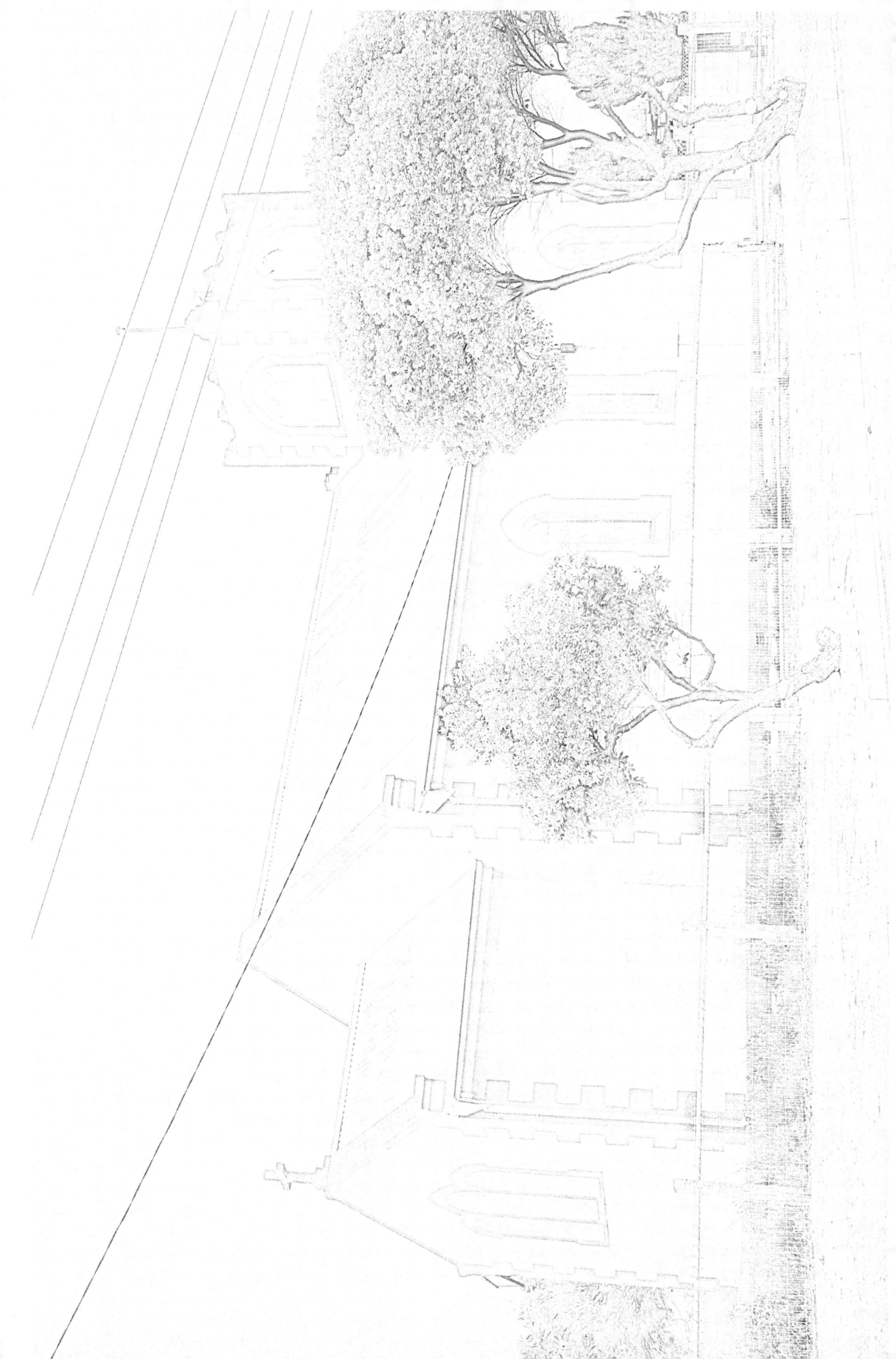

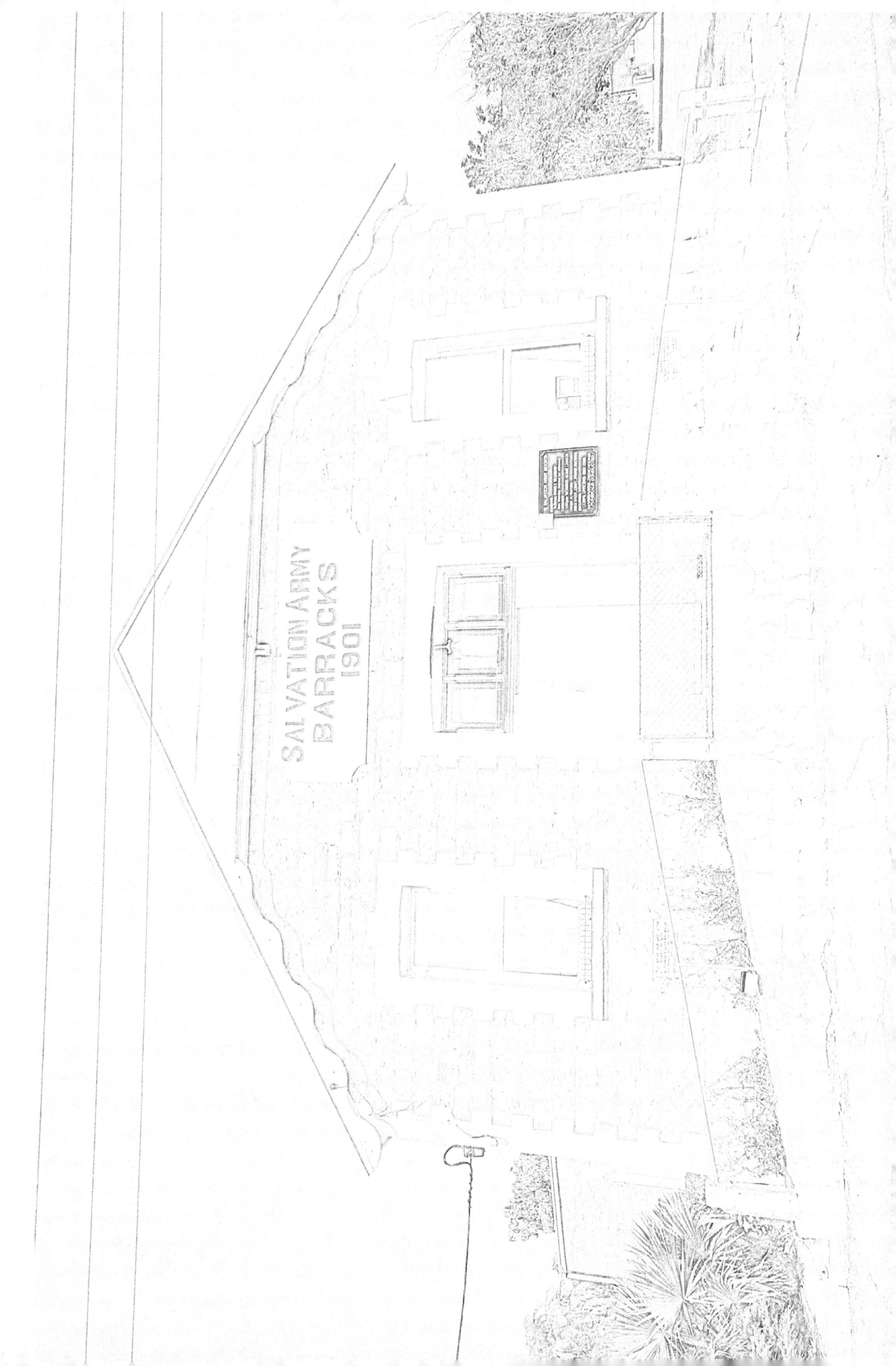

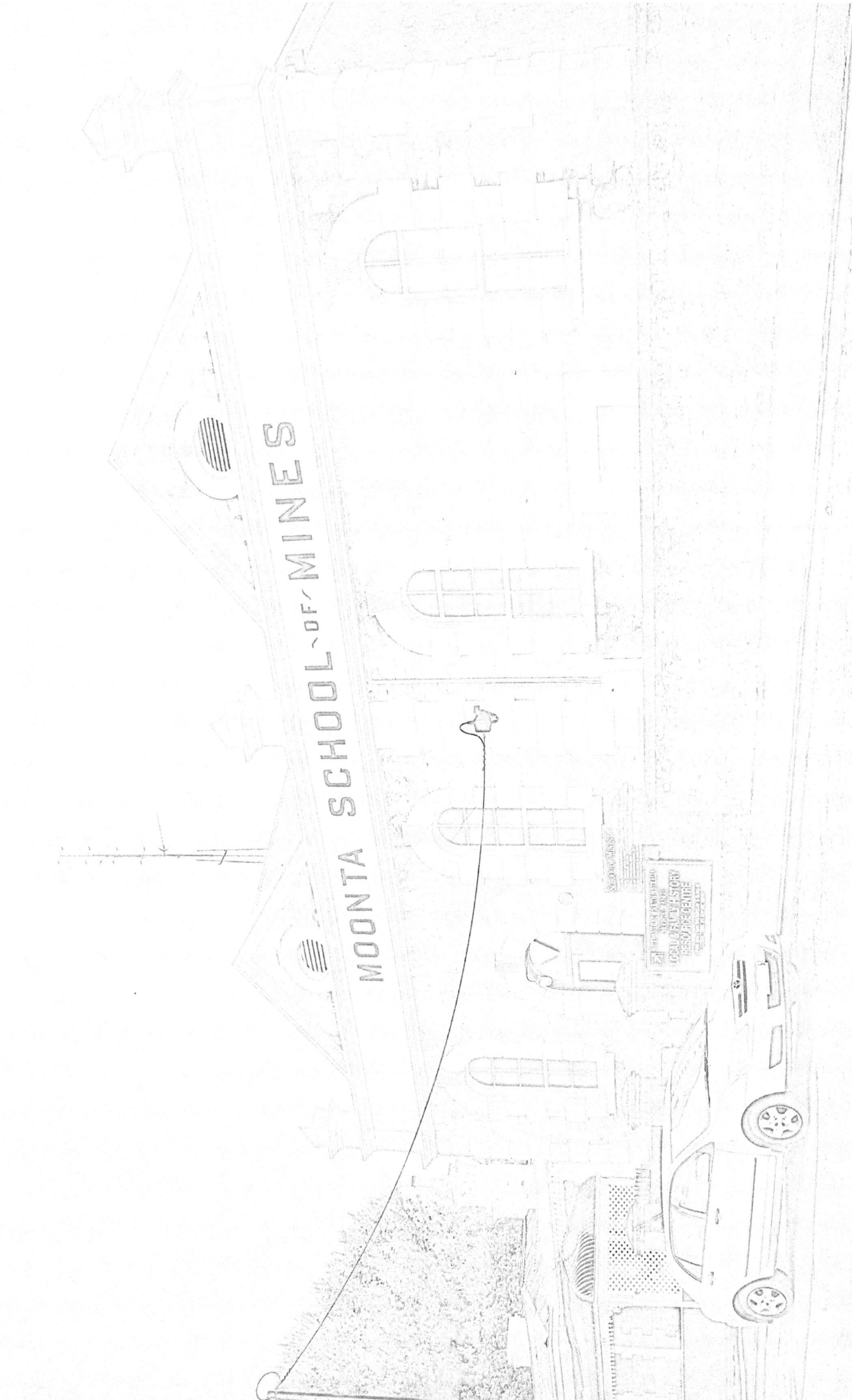

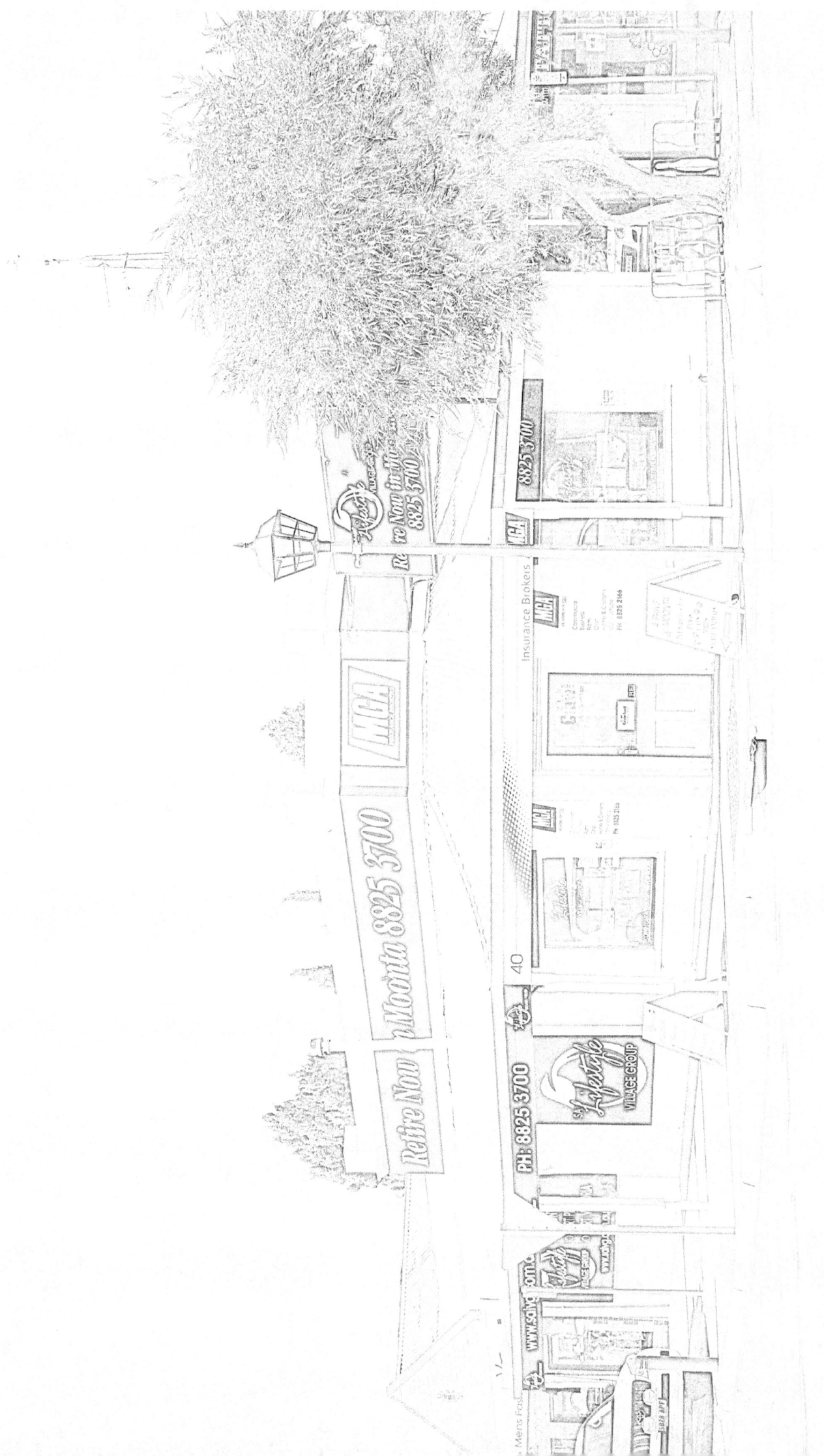

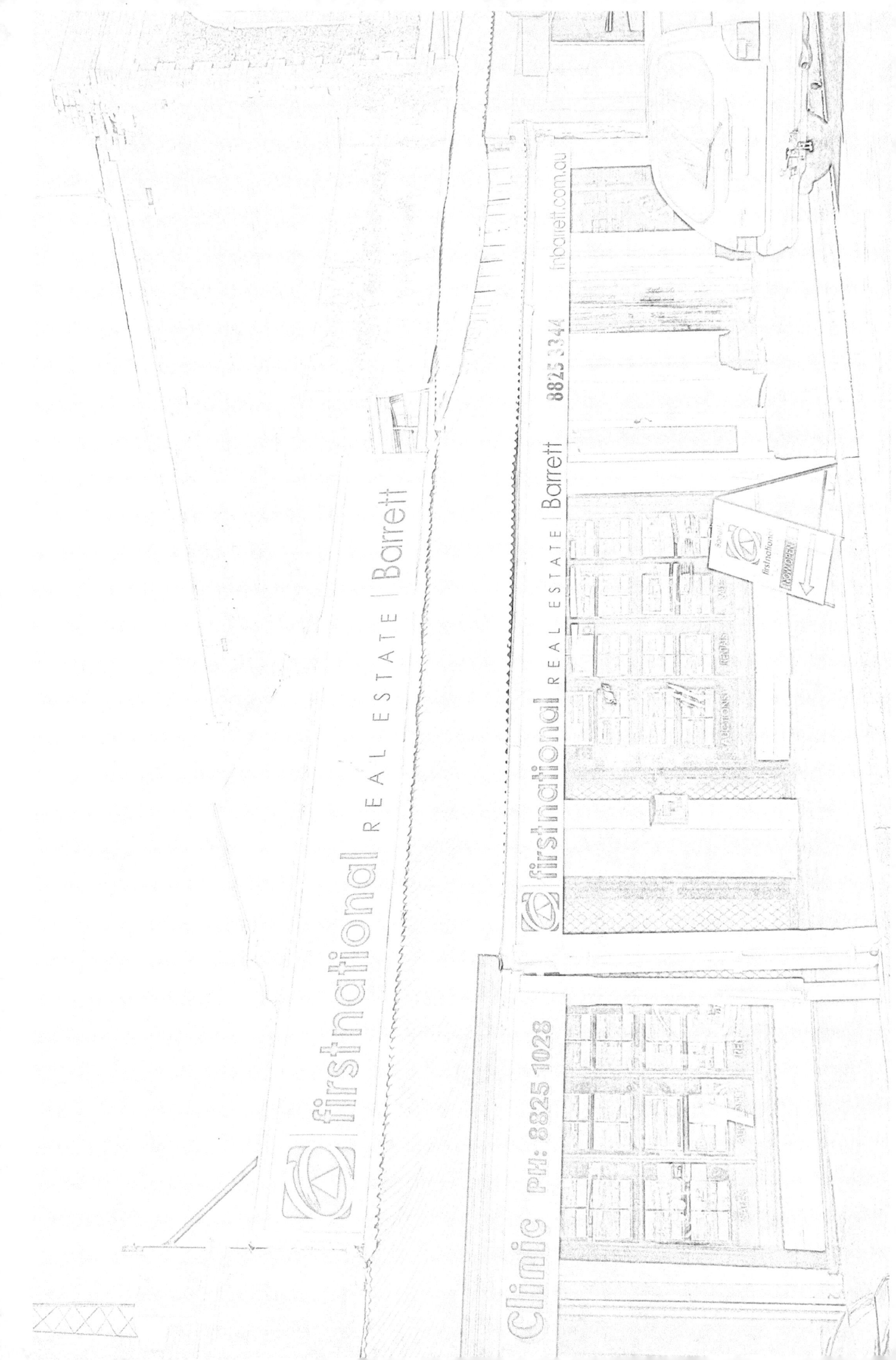

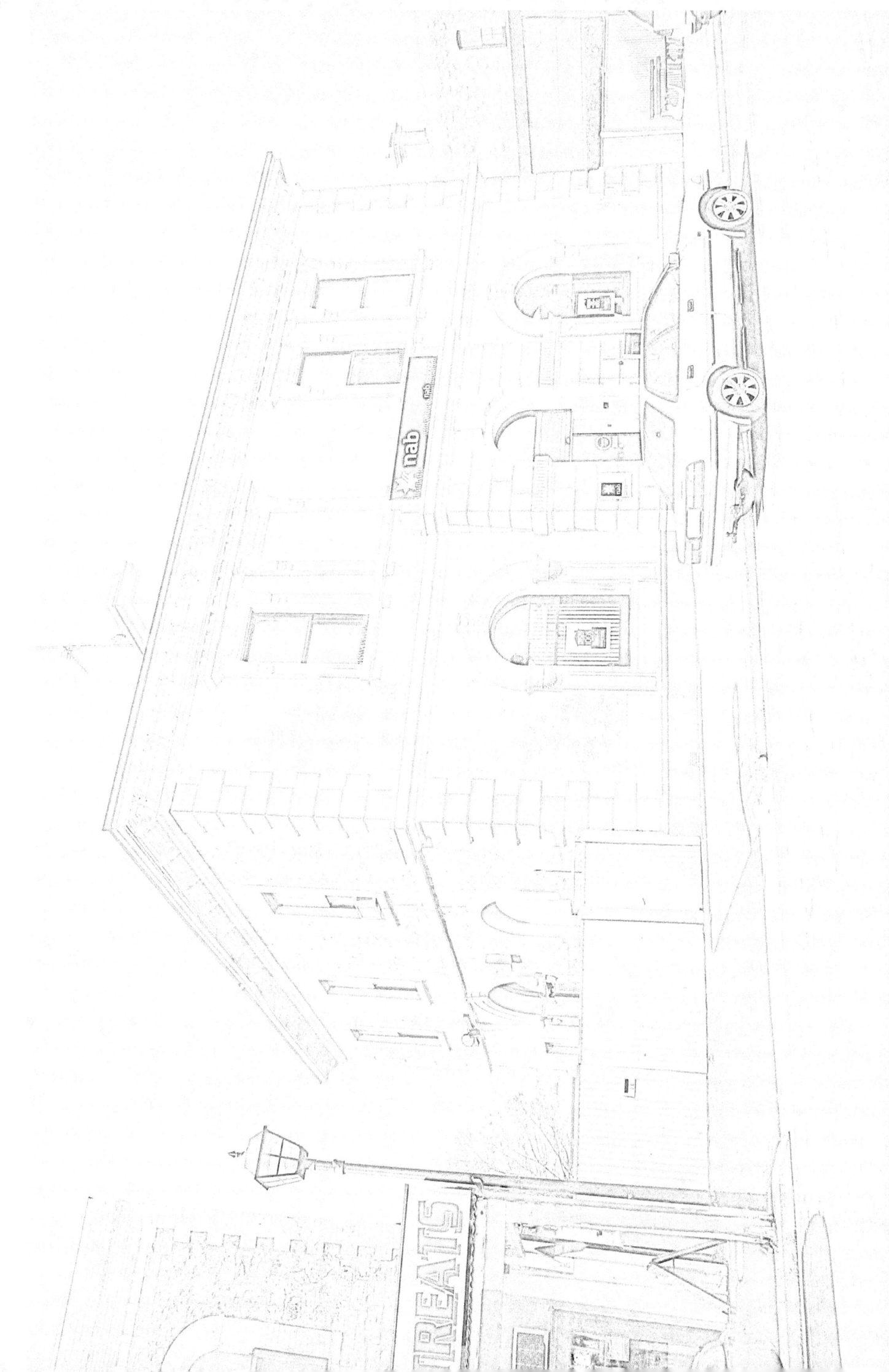

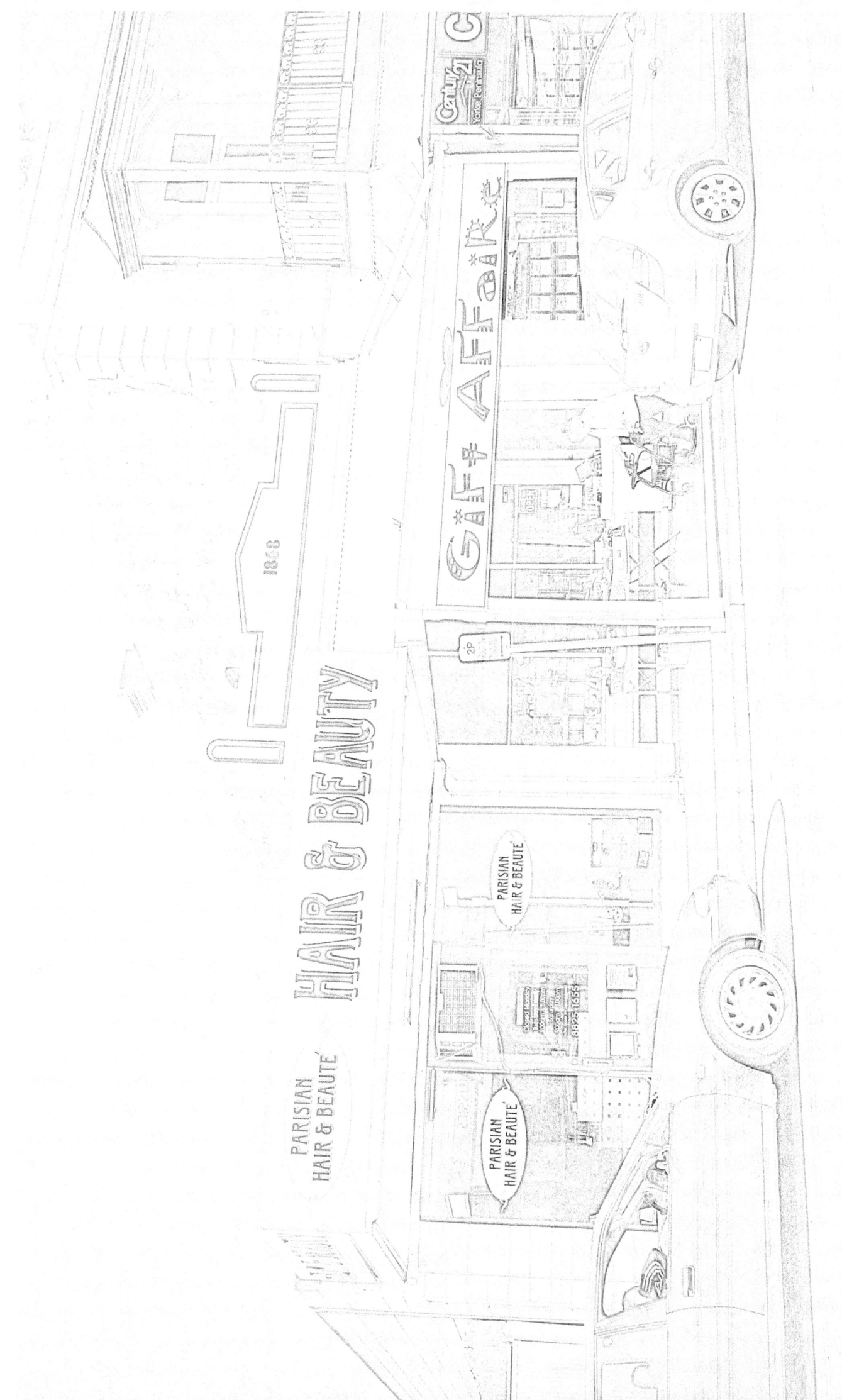

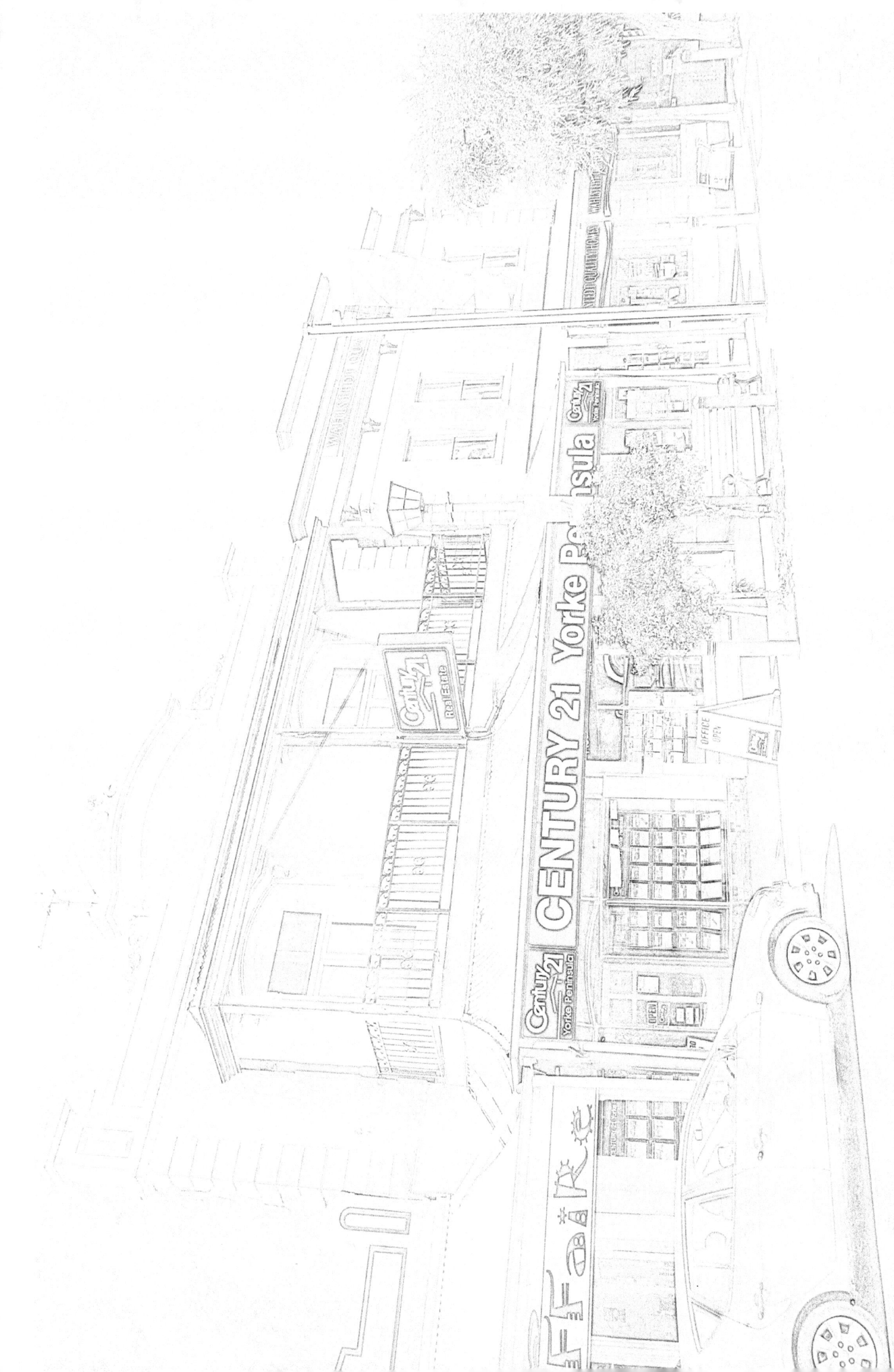

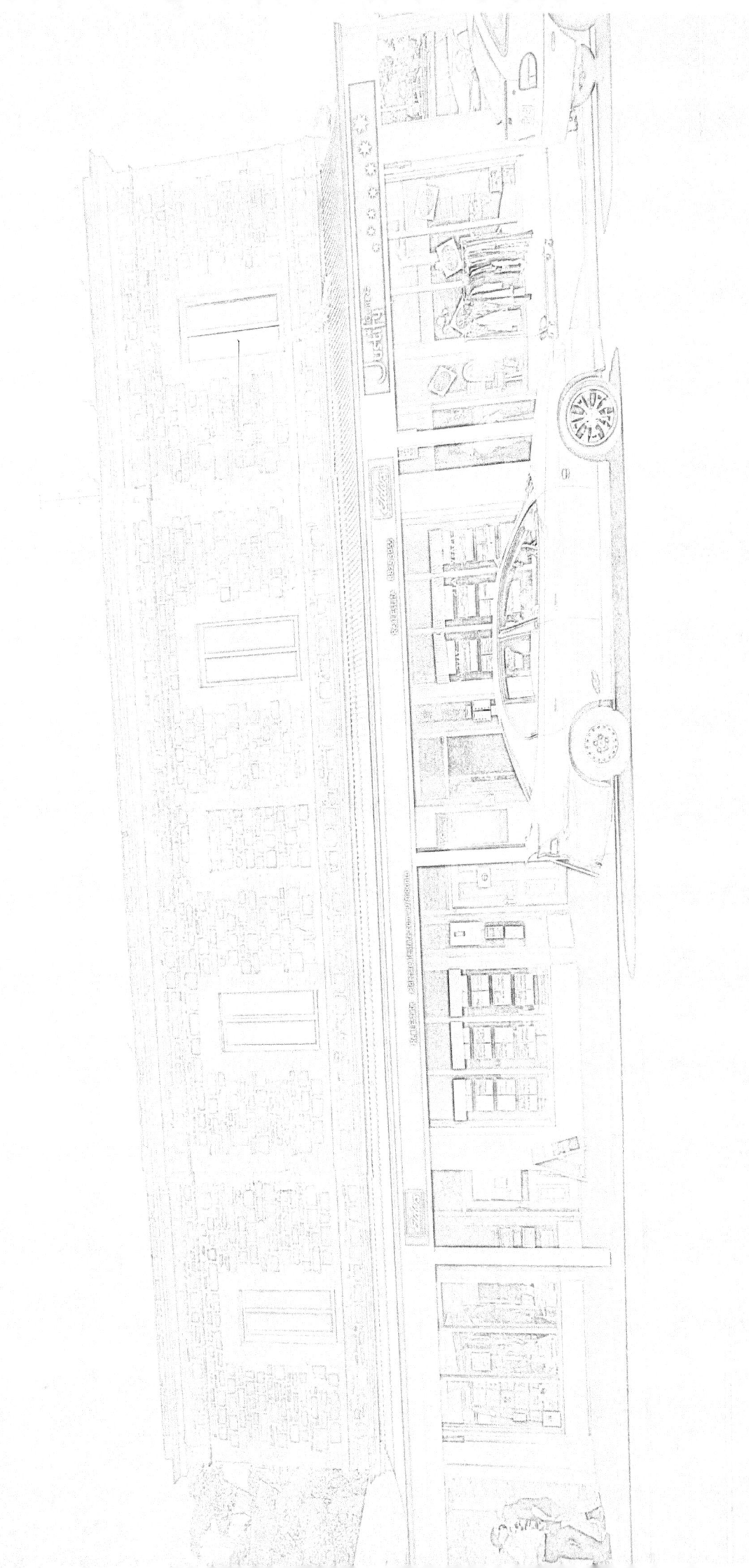

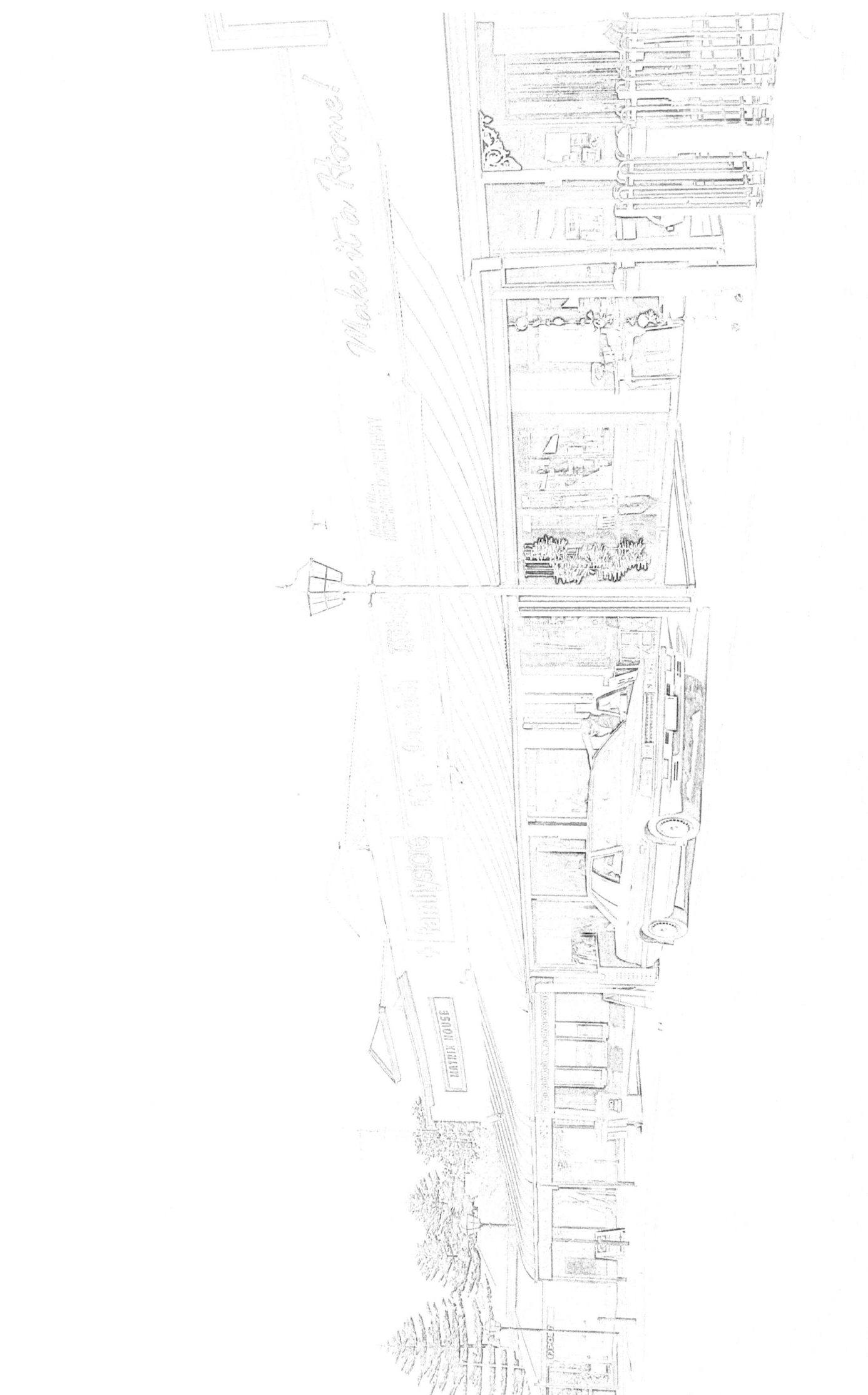